ADVANCE CRITI

I don't think I like her tome.
> --- *Jen Mann, author of <u>People I Want to Punch in the Throat</u>*

Where shall I start? It's filled with reprehensibly foul language, vulgarity, racial slurs, sexism, ageism, blasphemy, bestiality, gluttony, body-shaming, perversions, violence, pornographic imagery. The list is endless. That said, I really enjoyed it.
> ---*Governor Martin O'Malley*

Trailer Dogs is clearly a tool of Wall Street. And by the way, I hated the damn thing.
> ---*Bernie Sanders*

When the check for $250,000 clears, I plan to read this book, and then, if possible, schedule a symposium to promote the author's ideas and methods for wealth creation among the rich and powerful.
> ---*Hillary Rodham Clinton*

The hag that wrote this is a disgusting fat pig loser with a face like a brick. Her book made me so mad, I had blood coming out of my…whatever. If we're going to make America great again, we shouldn't teach our females how to read and write.
> ---*The Donald (Jan. 2016)*

I was mildly disappointed that the author didn't explore in greater detail how the ancient Egyptians used pyramids for grain storage, or why in hieroglyphics their heads are all pointed in the same direction.
> ---*Dr. Ben Carson, author of <u>Gifted Hams</u>*

I've been saying all along that the author of this book is a good-looking woman. I'd date her in a New York minute if my daughter wasn't available.
> ---*Donald J. Trump (Feb. 2016)*

Trailer Dogs contains off-colour jokes. Indeed, it is blasphemous. It is a veritable sewer, filled with marginally false information about Canadians. There were a few decent parts about corn holing, but not enough detail to sustain my interest.

---Canadian Senator Ted Cruz

I fail to see the humor.

---Carly Fiorina

The way I'm misquoted in the media is disgusting. The woman who wrote this book is a disgrace. She should be locked a cage with Chris Christie, and shipped to someplace really crappy, like Oklahoma or Iowa…or maybe Wisconsin.

---President Elect, Donald .J. Trump (June 2016)

Sometimes I think her skull is made of kryptonite.

---Spouse

TRAILER DOGS

Life in America's New Middle Class

Ellen Garrison

2016

TRAILER DOGS –Life in America's New Middle Class,
written by Ellen Garrison

Nomad Dogs Publishing

Copyright © 2016 by Ellen Garrison
Cover design by Ellen Garrison
Illustrations by Ellen Garrison

All rights reserved. Non-commercial interests may reproduce portions of this book without the express written permission of Nomad Dogs Publishing provided the text does not exceed 500 words

TABLE OF CONTENTS

AFOREWARD

PROLOG

ABOUT THE AUTHOR

CHAPTER 1
WHAT THE HELL IS A TRAILER DOG?

CHAPTER 2
WHAT IN GOD'S NAME WOULD POSSESS SOMEONE TO WRITE THIS STUFF?

CHAPTER 3
THE RESORT

CHAPTER 4
DOGS IN THE HOOD

CHAPTER 5
TRAILER GODS

CHAPTER 6
THE TRAILER DOG DIET

CHAPTER 7
AMY SCHUMER'S PANTIES

CHAPTER 8
OPRAH'S FEET

CHAPTER 9
TRAILER DOGS: THE MOVIE

CHAPTER 10
MY OLD MAN

CHAPTER 11
THE FOURTH ESTATE, DOG STYLE

CHAPTER 12
THE BIG STINK

EPILOG

AFOREWARD

An AFOREWARD, as I understand it, is a message from the author about what readers can look "aforeward" to in the coming pages. Despite what you may be thinking, this Aforeward is not a stalling device to let me ramble on and on and on about nothing until I organize all my rants into a book that people will enjoy so much, they'll recommend it to their friends and fellow book club members.

Trailer Dogs will enlighten you about a large segment of the American population you didn't even know existed, but which has been around since Ronald Reagan. The Gipper was America's first "walker" president. He roamed the halls of the White House at night looking for brains to snack on and trying to remember where he left his musket. He was unsuccessful on both counts.

In addition - and I think the more scholarly (brainiac) readers among you will be nodding in agreement – putting an Aforeward in one's book gives it the ***appearance*** of gravitas (substance) without condescending (talking down to) the reading audience (you people) or insulting their intelligence (smarts) outright (here and now).

Before you go patting yourselves on the back for being so clever, dig this: my old man, who boasts that he's my "manager" and is therefore entitled to 20% of the profits from ***Trailer Dogs***, claims "Aforeward" isn't even a real word. He says that's why the squiggly red line appears under it every time I type it. But regardless of whether "Aforeward" is an actual word or not, let's get one thing straight:

My old man isn't getting 20% of shit.*

As I prepare to begin penning ***Trailer Dogs***, it occurs to me that nobody writes much anymore. Nobody writes letters, or even postcards when they go on vacation. Rich folks, like the Mitt Romneys, tie their helpless dog to the top of the family Rolls Royce and go gadding about the world without so much as dashing off a single "Wish you were here" or "Having a great time hiding our millions in the Caymans" on the back of a card.

The truth is, a lot of people fall into one of two categories these days: Too damn rich and lazy to care about keeping in touch, or too broke and overworked to even ***think*** about taking a few days off from their Walmart greeter jobs to go on vacation and send a cheery postcard to their co-workers. If they're going to dream about something improbable, it's that their crappy Ford pickup will start two mornings in a row without them having to borrow their neighbor's jumper cables, and/or their neighbor's own crappy Ford pickup.

Apathy, privilege and wealth don't produce a best-selling book, unless you're a billionaire running for president of the United States and hire a hack to make up shit about how human-like and caring you are in real life. Authors like myself don't let our laziness, apathy or even interrupted cash flow stand in the way of writing a book. Like in the theme song from the Monkees' TV show of the 60's and 70's, ***we've got somethin' to say***, and we're going to say it.

Some of us, unfortunately, are no-talent losers, who write the dumbest crapola you can imagine. Many desperate charlatans, or so I've been told, self-publish their hokum bunkum with succor from a thesaurus, and a website that I'm going to need to reconnoiter anon.

While we're on the subject of boring books that sold a lot of copies, there was that famous Russian guy who wrote a book about war and peace, which somebody told me-and I quote: "… is the worst fucking book ever." Personally, I haven't read it, and who would want to after a terrible review like that? I honestly believe that Russians shouldn't be allowed to write books. I can't be the only one who hated ***Dr. Zhivago*** and Omar Sharif, with his giant, buggy eyes.

Russians consistently write about places so cold and so desolate, they'd freeze the balls off a Yeti. The main characters in their books are always relentlessly picked on and unfairly persecuted by a fascist government even genuine American heroes like Mel Gibson and Bruce Willis couldn't bring down on their best day.

And how about Valdemar Putin? Isn't he one of the meanest looking sons of bitches you ever laid eyes on? He looks like a snake (with an awesome human torso), and he had some guys poisoned. So, he goes and writes a book about judo, and Bob's-your-uncle, it's selling pretty well on Amazon. I rest my case.

*An email exchange I just had with my old man:

HIM: BTW I did identify that *aforeward* is a word, very infrequently used in literary circles. It doesn't pass my spell check (well Microsoft's spell check) but it can be googled. so I stand corrected.

ME: *LA DE FUCKIN DAH*
PS You're still not getting 20% of shit.*

*The little star next to "shit" means see the bottom of the page for more information about this topic. Maybe I should have put the emails up there where I was talking about that 20% shit. Well, too late now.

PROLOG

The AFOREWARD was probably too long, but I still haven't found that website about how to write and publish your own book, so I decided to add a PROLOG to give you even more valuable information about what's coming up in ***Trailer Dogs.*** Hopefully, this will also put to rest any crazy ideas you may have about demanding a refund. God willing, I'll be able to find that website soon, and won't have to add a Preface after the Prolog. Oh, and before I forget, I drew all the pictures for ***Trailer Dogs.*** I could have hired somebody to illustrate it for me, but they'd have expected to be paid.

To continue, it is estimated by me that approximately 5 million Americans ***would not*** want to live, as me and my old man do, in a travel trailer roughly the size of Kim Kardashian's ass (if our trailer's slide outs were extended on both sides). This figure does not take into account 5 million adult males who would, according to my extensive experience in the matter, be thrilled to live inside a dead mule's ass if they didn't have to pay rent, cook, or pick up after themselves.

Ergo, there are 5 million people who would not want to live in a trailer of any size, even if it was filled with chocolate bacon and Ryan Gossling sex tapes; and there are 5 million guys who would ***love*** to live inside a trailer, or an ass, whether it belonged to Kim Kardashian or a dead mule. Looks like a wash to me. If nothing more, these wholly verifiable statistics point out my deep respect for Kim Kardashian's ass, and its Zelig-like ability to turn up just about everywhere on the internet.

Now that I found that DIY book publishing site and made my old man read it, I can drop this Prolog and Aforeward crap, and cut right to the heart of the thesis behind **Trailer Dogs.** But before I get totally serious, consider this:

America is experiencing a mass awakening to the fact that its people are really pissed off over just about everything. Mostly it's because we've been screwed over so much with false hopes and promises. First, it was being led to believe that Santa would answer our wish list and bring us a lot of toys at Christmas - assuming we were good little boys and girls, and if we obeyed our parents.

Then we were told that if we trusted in him, God would answer all our prayers and give us eternal life, providing we were good, and if we obeyed the Ten Commandments.

As adults, we were tricked by politicians into thinking if we were good and decent citizens, and if we worked hard and obeyed the laws they made up for our benefit, we could live the "American Dream," and would be able to adequately provide for our children now, and ourselves, when we grew old.

Today, a majority of Americans still have faith in God, and a few have even retained a childlike belief in Saint Nick, or at least his spirit. But with very few exceptions, we have completely lost our faith in the American political system and our lawmakers.

One of the best indications of the prevalent unrest was a bumper sticker I saw during the presidential primary:

Bernie 2016
Because fuck this shit

I had an even better idea for a bumper sticker that will save on ink:
Fuck this shit

WARNING: BEWARE THE DOG

For the sake of argument, let's say you read **Trailer Dogs** and then start thinking about suing me over something you didn't like, or that hurt your fee fees. Well, here's the deal. You're up shit creek if you go that route. Me and my old man don't have any money for you, or your greedy lawyers. When they find out there's no $$$ in it for them, those shysters will drop you like a hot potato. Then they'll send you a big bill for the consultation, or take it out of the $20K retainer you handed over before they even let your whiny ass in the door. So, the joke will be on *you* for trying to step on my First Amendment rights. You should be ashamed of yourself for causing me to have to write this kind of crap in the first place.

And anyway, even if me and my old man *did* have lots of money, we'd spend it on a huge trailer with two air conditioners and a satellite dome on top. Then we'd travel around the country, adopting homeless dogs, and maybe even buy two more big trailers so we could adopt some cats and horses and some more dogs.

Furthermore, if you think any of the persons in this book resemble living or dead people, I should sue *you* for being so dumb, because it's just a coincidence and nothing more. Seriously, folks, would a Wharton-educated candidate for President of the United States like Trump be such a radicalized asshat that he would say or tweet the kind of bullshit you read in here? Does Amy Schumer really wear granny panties and think they're Extra Small? Get Real.

Likewise, to those of you who are contemplating posting a scathing review of ***Trailer Dogs*** and getting all high-horse farty mouth over the profanity in it, I have one word for you: STFU. I will review *your* review, and believe me, my review will kick your review right in its fucking balls.

So consider yourselves warned.

And don't be threatening my dogs either.

That is all.

ABOUT THE AUTHOR

In most books, flattering information about the author comes at the very end, after the Glossary and what have you. A lot of times a reader never gets that far, because the book is so crappy and poorly written that she stops reading and sends it to her sister-in-law for a birthday gift.

I'm pretty sure that won't happen with ***Trailer Dogs***, because your sister-in-law is a real dumbass. (Otherwise she wouldn't have married your dufus brother.) Nevertheless, I thought you should know a little something about me right away, so I insisted on putting ***About the Author*** here, in the front of the book.

To avoid being accused of gratuitous self-promotion, I asked my old man to compose an unbiased thumbnail sketch of me - ***in his own words***. He said he'd do it, and I was happy to oblige him.

Since many of you have memory and comprehension problems due to advanced age and abuse of prescription drugs, I felt it necessary to make this brief clarification before you move on to ***About the Author.****

Thank you, and don't forget to take your medications!

*See next page

ABOUT THE AUTHOR

Fetching, in a tight tee shirt and high-cut denim shorts, the author of **Trailer Dogs** reclines, youthful and voluptuous, upon a webbed lawn chair outside an older 5th wheel RV, parked on a concrete pad in a mysterious trailer park, which may or may not be populated with vampires.

She wears a wide-brimmed sunhat made of woven straw, framing an extraordinarily attractive face. She greets me with a husky, sensual Sofia Vergara voice, minus the ball-busting screech Vergara, as Gloria Pritchett, sometimes uses on the **Modern Family** TV show when she reprimands her unattractive husband, Jay Pritchett, played by Ed O'Neill, who is marvelously talented, but really hard on the eyes.

"Hi there," the author purrs, slurping greedily from a full size travel coffee mug with a bright red lipstick smear surrounding its firm, thickset nozzle. She crosses slender, tanned ankles, and takes another robust tug at the mug's hard, plastic nipple.

"I declare, Fat Daddy, it surely is wahm out today," she drawls, fanning her ample bosoms and wiggling her long monkey-toes atop high-arched feet, a sheen of sweat gleaming on her toe knuckles like summer dew drops on rose petals.

"You don't seem like the kind of girl who was born to the life of a Trailer Dog," I postulate observingly. "Willst you share with me what tragedy ensued that you became one of them, such as you write about in your best-selling book of the same name?" I ask questioningly.

"It's difficult for me to express without weeping copiously, but thank-you for asking, nonetheless," she croons, dabbing at flowing tears with a crisp white napkin that sprang from the corners of her lovely, almond-shaped, green, orbs. She circles already moist lips with a tiny, probing pink tongue, and gently places the now-empty coffee mug on a small patio table next to the lawn chair upon which she is reposed, legs playfully splayed asunder.

"Please continue," I encourage her. "I realize this is a humiliating subject for you, but it's important that readers understand the insanity that shut down the US government and destroyed so many formerly thriving small businesses like yours and your much-older husband's, only because assworms like Mitch McConnell wanted to bring down the first African-American president. Do you agree?"

Tapping her wrinkle-free forehead with clasped, liver-unbespotted hands, the author nods viagraously. Her large firm breasts strain at the snug tee shirt. Suddenly she slumps in her chair, overcome with grief and anguish over something – perhaps her many disappointments - perhaps the emptiness of her travel mug. "Let me obtain for you more beverage to glug down," I suggest. "Mayhap that will help."

Retrieving the travel mug from the chairside table, I hurriedly mount the metal step to the trailer. Inside, two small canines shriek and claw furiously, throwing themselves against the screen door as if to bar my entry. The larger of the two mongrels backs up slowly, emitting a low, cautionary growl from under a curled upper lip, displaying a row of angry white teeth. I eschew the raging upstarts as I shuffle over to the trailer's diminutive kitchen counter, mug in hand.

Next to several empty wine boxes, I spy a tiny coffee maker. Curiously, the device is unplugged and heavily rimmed with lime deposits. It does not appear to have been used or valeted in many weeks. The persistent canines continue to straddle me, and thrust themselves against my hairy naked shins as I sidle back towards the door to break the terrible news. There's no easy way, so I come right out with it:

"You have no more coffee brewed," I blurt, trying unsuccessfully to extract the larger beast's teeth from my lower leg. "Shall I make a fresh pot?

"You ... have ... fresh ... pot?" the author asks, momentarily displaying a hopeful countenance.

"Sorry, mate," I reply, in an ad-libbed impression of Michael Caine, the has-been British actor who played a womanizing cad in the vintage film, **Alfie**. "The teapot is empty, but bloody 'ell, I'll just pop my bollocks over to buggering Starbucks and fetch you a latte."

"Are you fucking serious?" she responds, her voice suddenly taking on the quarrelsome tone of Sofia Vergara's aforementioned TV character, Gloria Pritchett. "Why would fucking Starbucks build a fucking café next to a fucking trailer park in the middle of fucking nowhere?"

"That, luv, is an excellent bloody question," I rejoinder.

Author's Note: Never would I have believed my old man could write this well. I may let him help me write a fictional TV reality show, like on National Geographic.

CHAPTER 1

WHAT THE HELL IS A TRAILER DOG?

I'm not sure why anyone would ask a dumb question like this, but since you already bought ***Trailer Dogs,*** and all sales are final, I will attempt to answer without further comment or unintended sarcasm. Simply put:

A Trailer Dog is a dog…that lives in a trailer

Now that I have given the question a little more thought, however, and after breaking for a protein bar and a quick check of our box wine reserves, I guess I should correct a slight misimpression I may have unintentionally fostered by unequivocally stating that a Trailer Dog is a dog… that lives in a trailer. To the contrary:

A Trailer Dog isn't necessarily a dog, and may not live in a trailer

A Trailer Dog can be any gender and most any species, including felines and humans, and possibly birds or gerbils, but not insects. I used "dogs" in the title simply because I have two of them and they live in a trailer with me and my old man.

A teacher once told me that if I ever wrote a famous and exciting book that people would be glad they bought, I should write about something I know. After discarding twenty or so pages about potato chips, I decided to write about dogs and trailers. If I knew something about ferrets, for example, then the title of this book would be ***Trailer Ferrets***. Think about that before you waste any more of my time with dopey questions that might cause me to mislead you.

As I have tried to make abundantly clear, Trailer Dogs, or whatever kind of animal they may be, don't necessarily live in trailers. Some may live in Class A motor homes, manufactured park models, vans, cars, or a tent pitched in their parents' back yard. But by now, one thing should be obvious to you people:

Trailer Dogs do not live in conventional, stick-built houses

After a short lunch break and further consideration, I must again correct a misimpression on your part. To set the record straight, it is possible that some, perhaps many, Trailer Dogs live in conventional, stick-built houses.

I'm striving for accuracy here, so please bear with me. Some Trailer Dogs may live in conventional stick-built houses for part of the year. Come October, they hop into their cars or RVs and go someplace where snow isn't piled up to their cootch. These types of Trailer Dogs are often referred to as "snowbirds" or "part-timers" or "corn holing Canadians in a 45-foot diesel pusher."

Don't blame me for the xenophobia, folks, I'm just the messenger here. More on the corn holing phenomenon later.

Now we're getting somewhere. One thing I know about is living in a trailer with Trailer Dogs because, as I've been trying to tell you…

I live in a trailer, with dogs, and I am one myself

CHAPTER 2

WHAT IN GOD'S NAME WOULD POSSESS SOMEONE TO WRITE THIS STUFF?

People I'd Like To Kick In Their Anal Glands

In this chapter I will attempt to explain some of the many reasons I have undertaken the formidable task of writing **Trailer Dogs**. It's probably not what you think. Or maybe it is. What the hell am I, a mind reader?

Anyhow, I'm still shaking my head in amazement at what a great job my old man did back there with **About the Author**. Even though his writing style, as is clearly evident, is totally different than mine, his was a masterful portrait of me - the person who is now writing this part of the book about anal glands.

Author's Note: Anal glands are foul-smelling scent organs dogs have in their rectums, and which must be reamed out from time to time. (Like Congress)

While his profile of me was basically true, I'll be the first to admit that my old man might have gone a teensy weensy bit overboard comparing me to the lovely and talented Sofia Vergara, who plays Gloria on the TV show **Modern Family**. For one thing, I am a natural blonde, and I rarely raise my voice like she does all the time in the show. Plus, being a bona fide, legitimate American citizen, I don't speak the Mexican language in a phony, exaggerated accent, or dangle my gigantic tits in everybody's bowl of manuda soup.

Like I said, **About the Author** was fairly accurate, even though my old man (who, incidentally, reminds some folks of the geezer who plays Gloria's husband, Jay, in **Modern Family**) portrayed our dogs as a smidge more spoiled and vicious than they truly are.

It is a fact that I treat my dogs like they're my children, because frankly, they're a lot better looking and better mannered than most of the slack-jawed Honey Boo-Boo types you see running wild around Walmart. And, as the "parent" of dogs, I don't have to bake in the blazing hot bleachers while my half-witted, Ritalin-deprived sons sit glued to the bench during halftime at a soccer game, mining their noses as if Big Macs & fries are just inches away from their index fingers.

I will be the first to admit that my "boys" occasionally lick my face, having just finished sanitizing their anuses with their own tongues, and they *do* piss on each other's heads a minimum of several times a week. But I ask you this: Is their behavior any worse than having your 30-year old son inform you that he's leaving his wife and kids for a 45-year old one-eyed pole dancer who performs under the stage name Layla Pussé? I thought not. And who's to say your human son and Ms. Pussé haven't already engaged in the same type of tawdry acts attributed to our aforementioned dog sons? Glass houses, people, glass houses.

This brings me to a candid admission I need to make about myself in order for readers to better understand the true reasons I am writing **Trailer Dogs**, which was made available to you at a very reasonable price.

Months after me and my old man were shoved face first into a Trailer Dog lifestyle by the worthless, no-good jackasses known as "our government," we realized that the trailer we'd just bought didn't have room to store the 10,000 some-odd-books we'd accumulated over the years.

When we lived in regular-type houses with more than one room, we always built bookcases or shelving for our books, even in the early days when the only construction materials we could afford were concrete blocks and a few sticks of lumber we found behind a neighbor's tool shed. Downsizing to a 29-foot travel trailer meant that either our prized books, or our two dog kids, Sully and Ben, would have to go.

We took a vote, and our dog kids won by a narrow margin on the third ballot. (Just kidding - they won on the first vote.) We culled out a box or two of our favorite volumes from storage and pawned off the rest at the local library. It took five round trips with a pickup truck, but the gratitude in the eyes of the librarian and her hunchback assistant made the effort, and my old man's subsequent double hernia surgery, worth it. Then we both bought Kindles.

One of the very first books I considered for my Kindle was **People I Want to Punch in the Throat**, by Jen Mann. The title alone matched the pissy mood I was in. After a really angst-filled year of unrelenting deprivations, I was itching to kick some ass, punch some throat, and heap guilt upon the architects of global warming and those I held responsible for causing our swift reversal of fortunes.

Despite its overly long and physically aggressive title, **People I Want to Punch in the Throat**, was extremely popular, and was selling like deep fat fried lard cakes at a Mississippi county fair. I felt such a kinship with the author, who was a self-admitted pushy, foul-mouthed lib…kind of like Amy Schumer, a comedian I admire, respect, and who I now feel a little sorry for in light of the can of whoop-ass I'm going to open on her later in the book.

Anyway, so enthralled was I at the prospect of reading **People I Want to Punch in the Throat**, I overlooked Jen Mann's career as a real estate agent, along with the fact that her old man is Chinese and probably related to folks who can't make reliable hardware or poison-free dog food to save their goddamn lives.

Honestly, you have to wonder why the Chinese are so keen on poisoning one of their seven food groups, but that is an argument for another day.

Of the millions of reviews I read about **PIWTPITT**, the overwhelming majority were wildly favorable. Only a couple stood out as less than positive, including one from a cave-dwelling stuffed shirt who whined and carried on that the book had too many gratuitous f-bombs and raunchy language.

Ignoring the minority of witless complainers, and putting aside my extreme dislike for Jen's day job and her nuts and boltless husband, I confidently hit one-click purchase. Within minutes, **People I Want to Punch in the Throat** magically appeared on my Kindle screen.

The book started out pretty darn good. I was sitting in my recliner, lmao and trying to hold in pee as I scanned the list of dipshits whose throats Jen *and I* wanted to punch.

Then I came to this one:

People who treat their pets like children

I read it again just to be sure. ***People who treat their pets like children***.

It was clear beyond all doubt that this passage was aimed ***directly at me and my dog children***. The words were so shocking, so hideously vile and threatening, I interrupted my old man's DIY pedicure and called him over. Pointing to the obscene statement on my Kindle, I asked for his unvarnished opinion.

"What do you make of this fucking shit?" I asked, not wanting to influence him one way or another.

As he read the hateful words, my old man stepped back from the recliner, his face as white as the toenail clippings now scattered on our faded purple carpet. "Can you get your money back?"

"Nope. No refunds."

"You thought about calling our lawyer?"

"He's not been answering my calls since that misunderstanding about the retainer check."

Studiously rubbing his grizzled, pock-marked chin, my old man contemplated the dilemma.

"I guess the only thing you can do then is write a bad review of the book and post it," he said, refilling my thermal mug from the now wheezing wine box.

I pondered his suggestion for a minute before noticing that my thermal mug was inexplicably empty again, making me wish I'd bought the 30-oz. size instead of the puny 18-ouncer. Putting my regrets aside for the moment, I returned to the idea of writing a negative review.

On the surface, my old man's notion sounded plausible *and* sane - write up a withering review and be done with it. "It could possibly work," I admitted. "There *is* a ton of unnecessary profanity in the book - a lot of reviewers pointed that out. And for her to personally attack *me* for no earthly reason…"

"Not to mention it was a really stupid thing for an author to do business-wise…insulting so many would-be fans like that," my old man reflected.

"You got that right," I agreed. "I mean…I could sort of understand it if she was just talking about people who treat their *cats* like children, but she really jumped the fucking shark, singling out a dog person that way."

"Well, she's obviously batshit crazy," my old man observed, shaking his shrunken head. "Didn't you realize that was a possibility when she said she was a real estate agent married to an Oriental? Maybe you shouldn't have bought her book in the first place."

"Yeah, well it's just like *you* to blame the whole goddamn mess on *me*," I shrieked, leaping from my seat and trying to express my intense anger without breaking anything.

"I'm the victim in all this, and you stand there and act like I should have known better than to buy a book by a closeted dog hater who just happens to be a real estate agent married to a Chinaman. And another thing…why should I waste my time writing a blistering, but amazing review that might backfire and cause even more people to buy her book just to see what all the fuss is about? That's exactly how Hitler came to power after everybody bought that book about his Kampf."

"All I know is that I believe in you," my old man winced, siphoning another pint off the wine box into my travel mug. "That's why I'm sure you'll concoct some awesome scheme to turn this catastrophe around, and, hell, maybe even profit from it!"

I took another long pull at the mug and sat back in the recliner, my brain wheels spinning. "You're probably right," I conceded, "but don't think for a second you're getting 20 fucking percent."

The Author's Muses - Sully & Ben

Mindless Stereotyping

Trailer Dogs, even freshly minted ones, are very sensitive to put downs and slurs from people who should know better. This character flaw seems especially true of writers, and I am taking special care not to venture down the same slippery slope of stereotyping based on what I *think* I know about other cultures and groups of people.

Just last night I was re-reading a favorite book of mine, penned by a famous humor writer, a homosexual I'll call "Bob Sedaris," when I came upon some profoundly disturbing dialogue I hadn't noticed the first two times I read his book some years back.

Bob had been unfairly criticized much of his life for merely practicing his sexual identity. In one chapter of the book, Bob wrote that *his own mother* once told him she was concerned that people might think he'd been *raised in a trailer,* just because he complimented a household artifact *she* thought was tacky.

I suspected that Bob's mother may have made the shameful remark simply because she believed he was a failure as a homosexual. Obviously, she did not think her son possessed the sophistication and good taste of successful homosexuals, who know a fake Saarinen dining table when they see one.

This new-found disclosure in the book cut me to the very quick. My disgust was not because Bob's mother, a resident of North Carolina at the time, had said something most ignorant, biased hillbillies would blurt out in a moment of "gol-dern" stupidity. It was that an educated man of Bob's literary stature, someone who'd experienced so many senseless attacks on his own self-esteem, had repeated such stereotypical tripe about people, like me, who through no fault of my own, had been raised or was living in a trailer.

Why did Bob allow such a hurtful comment about me to taint the pages of what was otherwise sheer literary genius? And how might Bob feel if I had written in ***Trailer Dogs*** that my mother once opined that ***people might think I'd been raised in a neighborhood steam bath***, just because I enjoyed a book by a homosexual? This didn't happen, of course. My mother wouldn't have dreamed of making such an outrageously provocative comment, and even if she had, I would never put something that egregiously offensive in my book.

It was even more surprising, because Bob had struck me as unusually considerate and caring, and he seemed to be one of the least pretentious queer writers around. I will be the first to tell you that his ability to spin a yarn compares favorably with one of America's most beloved and revered humor writers, Mark Twain. But I should point out that even Twain had the good sense ***not*** to write a chapter wherein Huck Finn gave Tom Sawyer a blow job and caught crabs from Nigger Jim. There are lines an author simply must not cross.

My point is this: No matter how loving and nurturing they are, at times, all mothers can be real judgmental assholes.

BREAKING NEWS

You may not like that I have pre-empted a regularly-scheduled chapter of **Trailer Dogs** for something not really pertinent to the issues herein, but Wolf fucking Blitzer does it all the time on CNN, and they pay him millions. Even if nuclear war were to break out in Vatican City, the network stiffs would trot old Blitzer out to report on a story they thought was more important:

"Elvis would have turned 92 today, folks," a somber Wolf would frown, peering intently at his notes. "We here at CNN offer our sincere condolences to his family and his many fans watching today, by observing a moment of silence… Now, back to Anderson Cooper, who's live on the scene in Rome. Anderson, what can you tell our viewers about the white smoke that's forming a mushroom cloud over the Vatican?"

Look, I realize Blitzer needs to earn enough money to keep up the payments on his botox farm, but Christ, CNN, haven't we all suffered enough?

To continue with really important breaking news, me and my old man got back from grocery shopping about an hour ago. While we were at Walmart, something happened that was so weird, you'll probably think I'm making it up like I believe I cautioned you I might a few pages ago. I swear, this is the unvarnished truth. But first, a little background.

You know how aggravating it is when an old person ahead of you in line at Walmart waits until the last second to pull out her bank card, and then she doesn't know how to enter the fucking PIN, so she fumbles around in her purse for the checkbook, and out fall 500 coupons that expired three decades ago? Then the old gal starts shuffling around like an extra in *The Walking Dead*, sorting through yellowed slips of paper with her bony fingers, wailing about how the Walmart brass are cheating her out of 5 cents off a goddamn bottle of Halo shampoo that hasn't been sold since 1972.

In the end, the store manager comes waddling over and approves the geezer's entire stack of worthless coupons, and awards her a $50 gift card just to shut her up and get her the hell out of the store before she has a heart attack or pisses on something. Well, that's sort of what happened to me today with a confused old crazy lady.

The woman in line ahead of us, probably in her mid-seventies, was exhibiting signs of impending violence. The reason for her extreme irritability was because her Easter ham hadn't rung up with the correct rollback discount. I pretended to be interested in the cover of National Enquirer and Lyin' Ted Cruz's extra-marital hijinks as I listened to her denounce the hapless female clerk and threaten to take her ham business elsewhere.

The young clerk, thoroughly intimidated and with chin aquiver, surrendered with a submissive whimper, and re-tallied the ham at a lower price. The triumphant customer, clutching the prized ham to her bosom, exited stage left, just like Sally Field after she won a pity Oscar for *Fanny Mae* and mistakenly thought it meant that we, the folks watching the Academy Awards on TV, actually liked her.

Me and my old man, who were next in line, moved forward apace. He swiped his bank card and punched in the PIN, and everything was going smoothly. That is, until the lumpy bagger boy looked at me and mumbled the dumbest question ever to be asked in the history of the universe.

Do you want me to put your cold stuff all in the same bag?

"Why, heavens no!" I (hypothetically) responded. "By all means, put the cold and frozen items in separate plastic bags so they can melt all over the goddamn car while we drive 30 miles back home in fucking 112 degree weather. Then tomorrow, when we have food poisoning, we can shit and puke in the extra Walmart bags."

The brazen stupidity of the question was an insult to my intelligence. It was mind bottling, to be honest. What was this jerk thinking? Did Walmart even **bother** to train its 5 bucks-an-hour baggers? I contemplated whacking the living shit out of the kid to teach him some respect, but thought better of it. He was staring at me with a hungry look on his face that reminded me a little of the homicidal alien cockroach in the movie, **Men in Black**.

I then turned my attention back to the sad sack checkout girl, whose bejeweled fingers were now poised over the TOTAL key. Fortunately for her, at the last possible second I remembered the price-match discount coupons I still had in my purse.

Reaching into my bag, I retrieved the coupons with such rapidity, all four went fluttering in opposite directions. It took several minutes for the snotty bastard in line behind us - with help from Cockroach Bagger Boy - to retrieve the scattered coupons. But when all was said and done, I had saved a total of $3.00, including 50 cents off from a coupon I'd clipped from the newspaper in 2005, but had hung onto for just this sort of occasion.

Then - and this is the horrific part you've been waiting for - as me and my old man were pushing our cart toward the exit, a deathly pale old lady with wild white hair, suddenly leapt into the middle of the aisle, blocking our path and threatening us with a small shopping basket. Waving the plastic basket dangerously close to our faces, she hopped back and forth in front of us, her glassy, crazed eyes gleaming with malicious intent.

"GET THE HELL OUT OF MY FACE," I warned her, roughly shoving the crone aside as I dodged her swinging basket. When I glanced back, Walmart's beefy security force had surrounded her. Her ghastly pale thin arms dangled limply at her sides, and her vivid red mouth, with only two front teeth still intact, was agape. The basket the woman had been using as a weapon sat tipped on its side, its contents strewn about on the floor.

Outside, as we walked through the parking lot, I breathed a sigh of relief and turned to my old man.

"Did you ever in your whole life witness anything more embarrassing as that crazy old woman?" He looked at me knowingly, and shook his shriveled head.

Safely back in the car, I quickly forgot the terrifying incident. Regaining my characteristically cheerful temperament, I started thinking about how I had pulled a fast one on Walmart, using that expired coupon.

I began to laugh. And I laughed and I laughed and I laughed some more. I laughed so long and so hard that I accidentally pissed myself. When we got back to the trailer, I had to take a shower and change clothes. But it was totally worth it. I felt as though I had conquered the entire Walton family.

In case you think I'm making up this story, my old man will verify its truthfulness below.*

The story about her pissing herself in our car the day before Easter is completely accurate. Ellen does not observe this holiday, however, and she probably didn't realize that a Walmart employee, dressed in an all-white Easter bunny costume and distributing chocolate eggs from a small basket, was greeting customers at the door.

Life Before the Morlocks Came

The loyal, non-litigious Reader has already figured out that I, your master-servant, was not always a member of Trailer Dog society, and that the Trailer Dog way of life was thrust upon on me by lying, incompetent evil-doers.

Many of the evil-doers colluded with blood-sucking parasites in congress to shut down the government for months while they figured out a way to keep Wall Street and Halliburton on Uncle Sam's payroll. To state outright that I hate these people would not be in keeping with my Christian values, so let's just say that I pray that God will burn and torture them in Hell for all eternity, and leave it at that.

In order to conjure up a visual of the evil-doers, imagine, if you will, the nauseating, repulsive, Morlocks, who resembled Mitch McConnell somewhat, and who lived underground in H.G. Wells' ***The Time Machine*** movie. The Morlocks were planning to eat Yvette Mimieaux and her kind until Rod Taylor (or maybe it was Rod Stewart) showed up in the nick of time to save them.

If ***Trailer Dogs*** is successful - and there's no reason it won't be since we've ruled out refunds and lawsuits - you, Dear Reader, will have helped me triumph over the Morlocks like Rod Taylor or Stewart did, and I won't have to get up at the crack of ten to write books and do research on this kind of shit.

Before the modern-day Morlocks took over, my old man and I lived in a fabled land, among people known as the American Middle Class. It was your land and it was my land, as Woody Harrelson sang about on ***Cheers***.

We Middle Classers lived in the lap of luxury, for back then we had assets, like split-level houses with expansive yards and plastic flamingoes standing on one leg next to the birdbath. Yes, in those bygone days, we might have even owned a few shares of Microsoft. We had amassed financial resources that allowed us to shop at Target and Fashion Bug, and send our kids to accredited Community Colleges.

In the America I once knew, I was able to choose my garments from among imported fashions, hand-stitched in faraway places like Mexico, and bearing labels with the names of has-been models whose post-menopausal whiskers sprang from fields of botox on their lumpy, siliconed jowls. I wore shoes of the finest leatherette, and once a month, my old man pampered our '91 Honda wagon with high octane gas, even if it cost $3.50 a gallon.

In those salad days, we shamelessly drank our wine from glass bottles that actually had corks, and we bought champagne by the case, because we could afford to splurge on expensive brands like Korbel and Andre, and not just at Christmas.

Our kitchen was outfitted with an untouched bread machine, a pristine smoothie maker, and stainless steel appliances from Sears' "Elite" line. When we dined out, as we often did, it was at Golden Corral or Red Lobster, where the menus and the ambience befitted our status as Middle Class Americans.

Back then, life was sweet and serene. I didn't feel the need to swear continuously as I do today, or drink as much. And so what if I did? It's really none of your business, is it? In that paradisiacal world, buttinski assholes didn't accuse me of being bipolar or vulgar or drunk, like they sometimes do now.

Back then, I called my husband by his real first name, and not "my old man" or "pally boy" or "dicknose" when he got on my nerves. Back then, things were different. Like I'm trying to tell you, that was life in Middle Class America **before** the Morlocks ruined things for us just so they could keep eating fancy French food, like Yvette Mimieaux.

After the Morlocks took over, we couldn't get loans. Why?…because we were middle class and couldn't prove we didn't really need the money. We had to pay taxes because we didn't have enough money to set up off-shore accounts like the Morlocks did. Why?…because we were middle class. We had to switch to wine in a cardboard box. Why? Because we were middle class and could no longer afford nine-dollar bottles of Korbel, even at Christmas.

We had to shop at Walmart and Dollar General for our knick-knacks, our clothes, our food, our furniture—Christ, even our flu shots. Why? … because we were middle class and could no longer afford to buy clothing and get our healthcare at high-end stores like J.C. Penney's and Safeway. The discrimination against us was almost unbearable.

A Tragic Brush With Profiling

One eye-opening incident that stands out in my mind happened when I was almost mistaken for a felon. I was driving along in our battered old Honda wagon. Its tail lights were burned out, and the rear hatch was held shut with a bungee cord.

The Honda's muffler was shot and the brakes were dicey. Our plates had expired the month before. The speedometer wasn't working right, and we didn't have the money to get it fixed. At the time the near-tragedy occurred, I was closely following a brand-new Lexus so I could approximate a reasonable speed that wouldn't get me a ticket.

The driver of the Lexus I was tailgating was a nice looking black guy. He kept glancing nervously at me in his rear view mirror, and intermittently tapping his brakes for some reason. All at once, a city cop darted up behind me from out of nowhere and turned on his flashing light. My goose is crocked, I thought, mashing the last of a smoldering spliff in the back of the ashtray.

To my amazement, the cop pulled around on the left and swerved back in front of me. I jammed on the Honda's shitty brakes just in time to avoid rear-ending his cruiser. Lights still flashing, he motioned the driver of the Lexus to pull over.

As I slowed to avoid running over him, the cop, who was now out of his car, gun drawn, was approaching the Lexus with extreme caution. In my rear view mirror I saw the black guy, dressed in hospital scrubs, get out of his car, both hands in the air. He was shaking like a leaf and so was I. But I breathed a sigh of relief. Perhaps not all was lost to middle class Americans after all. Perhaps there was still some justice left for us, and not just for the wealthy few.

But I was wrong, Dear Reader. In today's America, if you aren't too big to fail, you're probably too small to succeed. Whether you realize it or not, if you've been waving the old Star and Stripes and wagging your patriotic tail because you thought you were a privileged member of the American Middle Class, ***think again***. You're no better than a Trailer Dog, trying your best to get by, like me and my old man.

And *not* like that black guy, who thought because he was a doctor he could get away with reckless driving in a stolen car.

The Transition: Selling Our House

So anyhow, me and my old man now live in a 29-foot 5th wheel travel trailer (circa 2002). We used to live in a 2700 square foot log house the two of us built on 10 acres, but we had to put it up for sale when we started getting threatening letters from impoverished bankers.

The long-suffering financiers just didn't understand why we were impeding the distribution of their annual bonuses by not making our two mortgage payments on time. We had depleted our life savings trying to keep the business afloat and pay our employees during the devastating government fucking shutdown. Our backs were against the wall.

Taking the bull by the proverbial horns, facing the proverbial music, and throwing in the proverbial towel, we called up a local realtor, a "specialist" in our particular area, to see what the property was worth, and when would be a good time to list it. Armed with a $550,000 bank appraisal we'd gotten the previous year in a delusional quest to refinance, we met the broker, Danforth "Tex" Squall, a few days later.

Tex pulled up in our driveway in a white Caddy SUV. After a cursory tour of the house and a few disapproving grunts at the decor, he pulled a stack of documents from his leather satchel and spread them out on the dining room table. Directing our attention to charts with horrifyingly depressing numbers, gruesome colors, and red arrows (all pointing downward), Tex didn't pull his punches.

"Folks always think their proputty is worth a lot more than it really is," he told us matter-of-factly, brushing aside the bank appraisal like it was used toilet paper. "I'll probably have to advertise this place all over the country just to round up a few looky loos," he drawled, swatting ineffectively at Sully, who'd been sniffing at his pant leg, and who was now growling suspiciously under the table.

After he'd finished destroying our will to live, Tex scratched his thinning silver-haired scalp and offered a tiny morsel of hope. If we were *really* serious about unloading the property in our lifetimes, and if we were willing to drop the price just enough so the banks and the real estate brokers could suitably wet their combined beaks, well then, he just might be able to rake up a buyer. Side stepping a puddle of half-digested kibble Sully had regurgitated near his foot, Tex moved in the direction of the front door.

It could take six months or more to find the right buyers, he told us, but somebody out there might be crazy enough to make an offer on a place like ours if the price was right, he said as he was leaving. He handed us a listing agreement with a suggested asking price 100K less than the bank appraisal. Then he turned and started toward his Caddy.

"Nothin's sellin' out here in the sticks," he reminded us, stopping to kick a big chunk off the top of a mound of cow shit next to the front porch. "And even if proputties was sellin'—which they ain't—nobody wants to live on a spread this far from town. And hell, you got 2700 square feet here and only two bedrooms. What's the deal with that? Most folks nowadays want at least five bedrooms so their kids can move back in when they hit 40 and lose their dang jobs."

"What should we do, Tex?" I asked, fingering the edges of our worthless half-million appraisal.

Tex adjusted his belt buckle and scraped the dung from the toe of his snakeskin boot onto our porch step. Spitting into the middle of the now decapitated cow pie, he squinted at us from beneath the brim of his Stetson. He was sneering, not unlike Clint Eastwood in, well, just about any movie that asshole's ever made.

"You can do whatever you want," he shrugged, "But no way are you gonna be gettin' anywhere near that appraisal price for **_this_** place, what with it bein' out so far and all this **_bull taco_** mess in the yard."

We signed the listing agreement that evening and FAXed it to Tex at his office in town. Early the next morning he was back, pounding a For Sale sign into the ground at the bottom of our driveway. "You need to get on up there and shovel some of that cow shit away from the porch," Tex instructed, wiping his dusty hands on his jeans. "I got some folks coming to take a look around 10."

After a month of back and forth and threats/warnings (from Tex) and threats/screaming (from me), we accepted an offer from the second couple that had looked at the house. Their offer was 20K less than the asking price, but Tex had worn us down with his gloom and doom, and his horror stories about houses that went into foreclosure because their owners were too stupid and greedy to understand that the bankers and the real estate brokers were first in line at the trough. And those houses had been *way* bigger and nicer than ours, he added, tightening the screw…with more bedrooms and less cow shit.

The Buyers' agent sent over a massive list of things her clients wanted included in the sale price, and a second, even longer list of things they wanted done to the property before they made good on their low-ball, crap offer.

Most of the stuff on their To-Do list was achievable, but the list was so long, we didn't think we could possibly get it all done in 30 days before closing. My Old Man was commuting almost 50 miles to work every day, and I had my hands full sorting through all our belongings, donating household items to charities, and packing up the few sticks of furniture the Buyers hadn't insisted be included in the sale price.

Exhausted, I called Tex to suggest that if the Buyers wanted each and every item on their To-Do list accomplished, we might need to delay closing for at least a week. He was unsympathetic to our plight and railed at me on the phone.

"These Buyers are hoppin' mad and already threatenin' to back out of this deal! And if they do, then where will you be? Everbody would know what your price point is, and believe me, they'd go even lower if you got any offers at all. Nothin's sellin' out there in the sticks, and nobody wants to live in a little old 2 bedroom house with them cows crappin' on the front porch. You need to stop hemmin' and hawin' and GIT THIS DEAL CLOSED, PRONTO."

Fed up with his phony cowboy routine (we'd found out Tex was a native Pittsburger), we rebelled. That evening my old man called Tex and put the phone on speaker. "We just can't get all of this stuff done,

Tex," he explained politely. "If the Buyers won't back off some of things on their list, or won't agree to postpone closing a few days, then so be it. If they want to walk away from the deal, we won't try to stop them."

"Now, hang on there just a minute," Tex said worriedly. "Nobody needs to be walkin' away from no deal. You can't ask the Buyers to delay closin' - they won't go for that nohow. They's packed up and ready to go. In fact, they's been askin' if they can move in a week or two **before** closin'."

Me and my old man looked at each other across the table. Huh? This didn't coincide at all with what Tex had told me over the phone about the Buyers threatening to back out. I totally lost it.

"What in the hell's going on here," I yelled into the phone, "Just this morning you told me the Buyers were pissed off and ready to walk out on the deal! Now you're saying they're so hot to trot they want possession before closing? Fucking forget it."

"Now calm on down, missy," Tex said patiently. "No need to go cussin' on me like that. I think I can work somethin' out here if you just keep your britches on a second."

At that point my "britches" were practically in flames. "You listen to me, Tex," I told him, "if you don't get this shit straightened out by tomorrow morning, you can come and get your goddamn sign and stick…"

My old man's hand shot out of nowhere and snatched the phone from its stand. "Hey there, Tex," he said amiably, "We have to run now, but pardner, we believe in you. That's why we're sure you'll concoct some awesome scheme to turn this catastrophe around, and, heck -maybe even profit from it!"

I reckon my old man's faith in Tex wasn't misplaced. The house sale closed on schedule, and Tex managed to satisfy the Buyers by giving them his personal check for $200 so they could hire a handyman to finish the chores on their trumped up To-Do list.

And in the end…

The Buyers were happy with the once-in-a-lifetime fantastic deal they got on their dream house, along with the extra $200 they pocketed for touching up a few scratches on the back door.

The Buyer's agent was happy with the commission she had earned by phoning the Buyers every week to report yet another concession 'ol Tex had finagled out of the Sellers.

And 'ol Tex was happy too - with his cut of the commission for his masterful manipulation of the Sellers' misguided expectations, particularly those of the foul-mouthed, combative wife with the badass dog.

But the Sellers were the happiest of them all. Happy that they'd seen the last of cow shit in their front yard. And happier still that they'd never again have to deal with or speak to that phony asshole, Tex Squall.

Buying the Trailer

When it began to look like the house was actually going to sell a lot sooner than Tex predicted, we started to worry about where we were going to live.

We owned a tiny, 23-foot fold out camper that we'd bought after most of the front desks at motels on the west coast posted pictures of Sully and Ben with a big red international prohibition symbol stamped across their heads. *And those were ones that had special rooms for folks traveling with pets.* Anyway, living in the camper with the boys for any more than a week or two wasn't something we were keen on, and 100+ degree weather was only a couple months away.

We ruled out renting an apartment in town, mainly because of the harsh, unfair pet policies, damage deposits, and mandatory credit checks. With severely limited funds and heavy hearts, we started looking at used travel trailers on Craigslist.

There were all kinds for sale, some old, some newer, and some that looked like they'd been recently salvaged from radioactive waters near Fukushima. Some were for sale by owner, and others were available from RV dealers who'd taken them in on trade or consignment.

After looking at several rigs offered by cash-strapped private parties desperate to unload their decrepit, toy-hauling ball & chain, we found one that seemed to meet our needs.

The trailer was a 2002, 29-foot 5th wheel that slept four. We threw the dogs in the truck and headed to the RV dealership, not too far from our house, where the trailer had been consigned for $10,500. Dave, a fresh-faced young salesman, unlocked the trailer's door for us.

Inside, the carpeting in the "living" area and kitchen of the trailer had been replaced with vinyl strips that looked like real wood, and the cabinets were in decent shape. The day/night blinds were a plus, and there were two electric slide outs, one in the living/dining area, and one in the bedroom that substantially increased the living space.

The bathroom was up two steps, and contained a full-size glass-enclosed shower, and a toilet in its own little closet. The bed was a "walk around" queen with a foam mattress and a worn, fitted bedspread. There was a long dresser on the other side of the bed.

The rig's mirrored closet was a good size, and there appeared to be plenty of space for towels, bedding and supplies in locker size cupboards. Like most trailers of that advanced age, the kitchen was very small. It had a nice array of drawers, though, and cabinetry for storage. It also had sufficient counter space for my old man to unpack meals he brought home from McDonald's or Taco Bell.

Outside, the trailer's swirly decals were a bit faded, and its exterior had a few scratches and nicks as one might expect. The tires were good, and looked newer, and a large storage bin spanned the front from side to side. All things considered, we liked the damn thing.

So what if the carpet in the bedroom was faded purple and the edges of the matching wallpaper borders were curling up like thin purple worms? Who cared if the two recliners and matching pull out sofa were wearing tacky floral chintz? The wall paper borders didn't interfere with the integrity of the hull, and the recliners were comfortable. Indeed, they **rocked**.

Everything in the trailer seemed to work ok - AC, furnace, slide outs, refrigerator, stove, microwave, lights. There was no trace of leaks in the roof or signs of water damage inside, and when the awning was unfurled, it had no rips or tears.

When Dave left to tend to another customer, I scoured the trailer with my nose, determined to find mildew, or detect any malodorous, nauseating smells that would indicate the presence of an un-housebroken pet, conditions I was intimately familiar with and would not tolerate. Having passed my all-important sniff test, the trailer got my seal of approval. It was perfect.

Other than the amount we'd have to pay for it, the only other out-of-pocket expenses we'd incur on the trailer were the cost of a 5th wheel slider hitch to mount in the bed of our truck, a new sewer connection, and a potable water hose. With the money we were going to save by **not** having to make monthly mortgage payments, we could even afford to rent a storage unit to house our important records and sentimental knick knacks.

When Dave came back, we were ready to make an offer and strike a deal. "We'll give you $5,000 cash up front," my old man said confidently, "No trade in." Taking a step backwards, Dave tripped and nearly fell out the open door of the trailer.

"Ummmm…did you notice the new tires and vinyl flooring?" he stuttered. "And all the appliances are working fine. For its age, this trailer is in excellent shape."

Taking charge of the floundering negotiations, I inserted myself between Dave and my old man. "Yes, Dave, and we also noticed the incredible shrinking wallpaper," I said, pointing out the curling border on the walls. "And how about that awful bedspread? It smells like there might have been some pets defecating and vomiting in there."

Dave looked horrified. "The trailer belongs to an older couple, and I don't think they have any pets," he said meekly. "They're selling it because their grandson got himself into a little trouble and they need some cash to help him out. They're both in really bad health, so they're hoping it sells pretty quick."

"Well, hopefully they don't have any communicable diseases," I offered sympathetically. "Some of those new bacteria and viruses hang around forever, especially ones that come from animal feces or vomitus."

"I wouldn't know about that," Dave shot back, getting a little too huffy with me for his own safety.

We walked back outside, and Dave tagged along behind us. When we reached our truck, Ben and Sully's heads were hanging out the half open window. When Dave approached, the hair on Sully's back stood up, and an ominous, threatening growl rose from his little throat.

"He must smell my dog," Dave suggested, quickly snatching his hand back to avoid Sully's snapping jaws. "Anyway, I sure appreciate you folks coming in today, but I don't think the sellers will accept your offer," he told us. "Their trailer's only been here a few days, and 10,500 is a fair price..."

"That may be so," Dave, I wisely counseled the earnest young guy, "But you know, nothin's selling out here in the sticks. That trailer could sit on your lot for months while that old couple gets sicker and sicker. God forbid they should die before you get an offer. Then where would you be?" I started rolling the window up very slowly, waiting for Dave to mull over the big mistake he was about to make.

Dave scratched his head and circled the dirt with the toe of his boot. "You're probably right, ma'am" he agreed, "But we have some other folks coming to look at the trailer later today. I'll be sure and call you if we don't make the sale."

I glanced nervously at my old man, and hurriedly rolled the window back down. "You drive a hard bargain, Dave," I observed. "Listen, what-say we bump our offer up to $7500 and you agree to fix some stuff—like the wall paper and the bedspread—and maybe have the whole trailer cleaned and sanitized?"

Dave shook his head regretfully. "Can't do that, I'm sorry to say. The price is already so low, it's being sold 'as-is.' I guess I could take your higher offer to my manager, though. He gets back from vacation next week."

"But you just said you have more people coming to look at it today, Dave," I said, getting a little worried. "What if it sells to somebody else before your manager has a chance to approve our offer?"

"That's always a possibility…" Dave admitted, sadly hanging his head. "Godammit, Dave, I'm getting a little tired of this run around," I said, my sudden angry voice causing the shark's fin hair on Sully's back to rise again. "What if we settle on $10,000 and forget about the goddamn To-Do list?"

"You know, I just might be able to swing that," Dave conceded, the light coming back into his eyes.

I nudged my old man and winked. "Then it's a deal?"

"You bet," Dave replied, a wide grin appearing on his face. "I'll just need to take a $500 deposit before you leave." My head snapped around. "Wait just a minute, Dave. Didn't you say you'd need to ok any deal with your manager first?"

"I'll call him while you're making out the check in the office," Dave said, "I'm 100% sure it'll get approved." Breathing a sigh of relief, I dug in my purse for the checkbook.

"Oh, and Dave, don't forget to call those other people right away and tell them the trailer's already been sold."

And in the end…

The Buyers were happy with the once-in-a-lifetime fabulous deal they got on the trailer of their dreams and the extra money they saved after the foul-mouthed, but very clever wife bargained the asking price down $500.

The Sellers were happy because they'd seen the last of their crapped-in, crapped-out trailer, happy they could now afford a few more weeks of their expensive, life-saving prescriptions, and happier still that they'd never again have to bail out or speak to their cokehead loser grandson.

But Salesman Dave was the happiest of them all, because he could buy cocaine with the five grand his grandparents gave him for selling their crappy 5th wheel trailer to two gullible old shits with a badass dog.

CHAPTER 3

THE RESORT

As a rule, a Trailer Dog's domicile, whether on wheels or nestled on a flimsy foundation, can be found in a trailer or RV park. (And sometimes in the parking lot at Walmart.) Many of these facilities have the word "Resort" tucked somewhere in their names in order to entice less intelligent, gullible travelers and prospective residents. So effective is this false and misleading type of advertising, even folks like me and my old man may be lured in.

The "Resort" moniker may also be applied to RV or trailer parks located 20 feet from a freeway, with active train tracks running across the back of the lot. A giant plastic tub, filled with fetid water, is often referred to by the Resort's resourceful owners as "a spa." Veteran Trailer Dogs never go near the spa, other than to observe local wildlife (cows, javalina, raccoons) pausing to drink from its murky waters, or, in the case of the raccoons - to angle for a snack.

Some RV Resorts feature paved streets, valet parking, saunas, Jacuzzis, 18-hole championship golf courses, exercise rooms, laundry/dry cleaning facilities, bordellos, tuxedo rentals, gourmet grocery stores, a clubhouse w/libraries and IMAX theaters, as well as on-site master chefs, plastic surgeons, and mobile colon cleansing services. Even though I made up most of those improbable RV Park features, I believe it is only a matter of time before high falutin' Canadian snowbirds insist on such amenities.

Our Resort/Trailer Park is managed by Gretchen and Lloyd Bird, and their dog, Charles. I'm not sure who actually owns the place, because whoever they are, they don't make themselves known. Gretchen is firmly in charge, and she rules the park with an iron fist, which she occasionally uses to keep Lloyd in line. But more about that in an upcoming chapter. Meanwhile, let me tell you about a few of the Resort's amenities…

The Dog Pond

The swimming pool is smallish, but fairly nice. I only used it once, though, and haven't been back since. Five minutes after I jumped in, a yellow jacket attached itself to my right cheek and commenced to sting the living shit out of me. I rose from the pool and hovered in midair, making loud, unearthly noises like a leviathan surfacing from the watery depths of the ocean.

My right cheek swelled up and burned, and I felt light-headed and out of breath from all the screaming and cussing and flailing about. My old man (that's what us married Trailer Dogs call our husbands) hauled me back to our fiver (that's what us Trailer Dogs call our 5th wheel trailers) and put some Mitigator ointment on the sting to get the poison out. (That's what us Trailer Dogs call First Aid.)

Anyhow, when the ointment didn't help much, I applied a box of wine to my tonsils, and that helped a lot. The second application resulted in a cure. My throat was sore for several days from all the screeching and carrying on, and I contemplated a lawsuit against the party I felt was most responsible for my near-fatal experience. I later discarded the idea of litigation when someone told me I wouldn't be able to testify against my old man in a court of law. Now that I think about it, it was my old man who told me that.

I hadn't really wanted to get in that damn pool in the first place. On any given day it's crowded with Trailer Dog Geezers. TD Geezers hate to swim. What they like to do is suck booze out of discreetly lidded cups and float around on pool noodles all day. Reeking of sunscreen and BenGay, they spy on one another from behind Walmart sunglasses with tape on the nose bridge, as they wade around the edge of the pool a safe distance from each other lest they blunder headlong into a Geezer fart.

Most of the Geezers wear brimmed canvas hats emblazoned with clever sayings like "Gone fishin'" or some such shit. Next to actually swimming, if there's one thing a Geezer despises, it's the sun. And Adam Sandler. Ok, make that three things.

Anyways, I had a hunch that at least two or three of the Resort's Geezer Brigade were long-term Depends customers and droolers. So I wasn't too thrilled about hanging 10 in a vat of simmering Geezer noodle soup, chlorination be damned. But as he always does, my old man sweet-talked me into taking a dip by promising me an hour-long, post-swim foot massage afterwards, which I never received because he is a fucking liar.

I went online and bought a swimming top, with long sleeves, to protect me from the damaging rays of the despicable sun, and, hopefully, from Geezer leakage. I purchased an embroidered canvas sunhat, which I also never received, not because my old man is a liar, but because it was on backorder and I got pissed and cancelled the damn thing. At Walmart I found a bright orange pool noodle, and I bought 2 in case I misplaced one.

To make a long story short, my brief dip in Geezer Soup was a costly disaster. And although I haven't noticed any symptoms yet, it's very likely that I contracted a Geezer disease, like dementia, from that pool. At least that's what my old man says probably happened. But like I think I might have said to somebody whose name I can't recall, he's a fucking liar.

Billiards, anyone?

Another popular feature of our trailer Resort is the billiards table in the clubhouse. It's where crusty old male Trailer Dogs, in varying degrees of decay, congregate to shoot a little pool and practice their comedy routines about the corn kernels they found in their stool, and how an eggplant at the supermarket reminded them of their ballsack the day after hernia surgery. The camaraderie and good-natured teasing at the billiards table is sort of like **Band of Brothers**, only with an all-zombie cast.

What these old Trailer Dogs are doing is practicing their act for Taco Tuesdays at Pedro's Taco Barn. Once seated at two tables pushed together under a battered Dos Equis sign, a pink-haired waitress, younger even than their great-great granddaughter, will ask them what they'd like from the menu. That cues the headlining Geezer to pop back with a side splitter like:

"Sweetie, if my old lady would cut me some slack, I'd give you an order you couldn't refuse."

The other Geezers at the table snicker and bob their oversized, tractor-hatted heads, waiting in anticipation for a flirty comeback from Pinky. They cast side eyes, elbow each other, and muffle guffaws. Pinky, clearly not amused and in pain from her freshly pierced nose, shrugs and makes a tiny check mark on her pad. The check mark will remind her whose refried beans to spit in on her way back from the kitchen.

Pinky knows exactly how to deal with these assholes, because she comes from a long, distinguished line of Trailer Dogs. In fact, Pinky and her entire family live in the trailer park directly across the highway from her customers' trailer park. Her grouchy, misogynistic Grandpa Phil sometimes plays pool with these jerks, and frequently consults with them as to which convenience store sells the coldest beer. And many times, Pinky has felt compelled by her feminist inclinations to hock a loogie into Grandpa's whisky glass, just on general principles.

At Pedro's, a good time will be had by the early bird crowd until the clock strikes 5 pm and the price of the tacos and beer go up a buck. That's when the tightwad Geezers hitch up their drawstring stretch pants, conveniently forget to leave a tip, and head on back to the Resort to paddle around in the Little Pool of Horrors.

Pinky despises these guys. She's working hard and saving her money so that one day she can break free from this shitty, oppressive lifestyle, and move in with her boyfriend, Zach, who's currently living in a tent at the KOA. Maybe one day they will even be able to afford a dog.

Corn Holing

There's a horseshoe pit and a corn hole court at the Resort. I've never seen Trailer Dogs of any sort pitching horseshoes, but corn holing sure can pack them in, especially when the Canadian snowbirds come to town.

Maybe the cozy corn hole court and rough and tumble American Trailer Dogs are what lure so many Canadians to this particular destination during the winter months. Canadian Trailer Dogs have a deep-rooted passion for the sport, and won't pass up a chance to show off their well-honed corn holing skills to enthusiastic rookies.

There's no denying that Canadians are expert, indefatigable corn holers. Woe be to the casual American Trailer Dog observer should he linger too long after a corn holing match has ended. More often than not, he'll be dragged onto the empty court by one or more insatiable Canadians, and forced into overtime play.

Overtime corn holing, as I understand it, is even fiercer than regulation corn holing, and can result in "sudden death" losses by out-of- shape American Trailer Dogs who are not familiar with Canadian rules. By anyone's standards, Canadians out-corn hole any other nation, including professional teams from Greece.

Even though I'm not a big fan of corn holing or Canadians in general as a foreign, sadistic, sanctimonious race of job-stealers, and despite my feeling that a 500-foot great wall* must be built** along the US border to keep them out***, I will be the first to admit that when it comes to corn holing, Canadians usually end up on top of Americans.

*   *With barbed wire at the top and bottom*

** *Canada will be forced to pay for this wall with profits from their national corn holing events*

*** *Mexico has agreed to help defray the cost of the wall to keep Canadians out of Mexico, and to prevent them from turning the Sierra Madres into a drug smuggling corn holers' refuge.*

The Poker Club

In addition to the billiards table, the Resort clubhouse has a big round table where gray beard Trailer Dogs gather for their poker club on Saturday nights. My old man has seen twenty dollar bills change hands over a game of pool, but the poker pots are strictly penny ante, and the big winner never walks off with more than a buck or two.

You very rarely see a female Trailer Dog playing pool or poker, although these amenities were definitely established for the benefit of women forced to live in the confines of a trailer with their crackpot husbands. Were you to put your ear to any trailer door on any evening around 6:00 pm, you might hear the following conversation, or one very similar.

Mary:

Earl, are you going over to the clubhouse? Judy said there's a poker game tonight. Gil's going.

Earl, lacking the courtesy to suppress a long, rumbling fart:

Whelp, I thought I might just stick around here tonight and watch me some tube.

Mary, getting apprehensive:

There's that big flat screen in the clubhouse...

Earl, intensely scratching his groin area:

Yeah, but they always have it tuned into that Duck Dynasty shit, and it's the same thing every night.

Mary:

I'm sure the Duck family isn't even on tonight, Earl. Anyway, Gil's going to be there, and you know how bad he is at cards. You won almost 75 cents off him last week.

Earl, belching fondly at the memory:

Yep, cleaned him out with a bluff on a pair of deuces. Dumb ass.

Hey, do we got any more of them chips that taste like bacon grease and tumaters?

Mary:

No, you ate the last of those for breakfast, remember?

Earl, examining a mother lode of wax freshly mined from his right ear.

Shit. Well, I reckon that explains why my farts smell like a BLT.

Mary, throwing up a little in her throat:

For God's sake, Earl—

Earl, chuckling over the brilliance of his gross fart joke:

Man, I sure could use a cold beer.

Mary, lying through her teeth:

You drank the last one with your breakfast chips, Earl.

Judy said Gil was bringing a 12-pack to the clubhouse.

Earl, rising from his recliner:
Well, hell... maybe I'll just mosey on over there and see if I can screw old Gil out of another 75 cents.

Mary, sensing checkmate:
Have fun, babe!

As the trailer door closes behind Earl, Mary rummages in the back of the refrigerator for the hidden beer. She then retrieves the bag of bacon & tomato chips from a top kitchen cabinet.

Mary settles into Earl's recliner, and turns the TV to the Duck Dynasty channel.

The aroma of a BLT fills the air. Mary sighs.

It smells like…victory.

The Dumpsters

Four dumpsters serve approximately 125 Trailer Dog residents at the Resort. On Sunday mornings, when most Trailer Dogs are sleeping off a bender in church, local scofflaws sneak in to dispose of their worn out car parts and tires, undigested deer carcasses, and the pit bull shit they scooped up from their own front yards.

Sometimes, if the dumpsters are already chock full, the culprits will carefully place rusty broken axles and even piss-stained mattresses next to the dumpster for Trailer Dogs to pick through when they get back from their snake-handling events at church. That's what's called Quid Pro Quo, folks.

But this unexpected display of townie generosity often leads to spats amongst Resort residents, who are quick to exchange curses and air fists over contested ownership of an old suitcase with a broken zipper and no handle, or a pathetic arrangement of artificial lilies in a plastic cemetery urn, bearing a faded purple sash that reads: "Beloved Grandfather."

As if it isn't enough that Resort Trailer Dogs must endure the constantly overflowing dumpsters, aromatic with shit from dogs that don't even live here, Management has the gall to accuse us of crimes we probably didn't even commit. At least once a week, a folded sheet of white paper appears in all the residents' mail slots, with a message that goes something like this:

NOTICE TO ALL RESORT GUESTS

It has been brought to my attention that you are not cleaning up after your dogs again. I have personally inspected certain areas in the park and have found excrement of a medium size and fresh consistency.

This excrement IS NOT a product of the cows that wandered through the Resort last week when some irresponsible moron forgot to close the gate, nor did it come from the group of marauding Javalina that sneaked in and attacked Cal Larson's visiting aunt. This is <u>filthy</u>, <u>disgusting</u> dog excrement, and will not be tolerated! I will find out who is doing this, and I will personally write you up and fine you $250. If I catch you again, you will be asked to leave the park immediately and for good. YOU KNOW WHO YOU ARE!!!!!

Believe me, I have people and cameras watching you at all times. I will get to the bottom of this and persecute you to the letter of Resort Rules. You know I mean business! I have done it before. Clean up after your dogs and dispose of the waste in the dumpsters conveniently located throughout the Resort.

Lastly, if you see anybody who doesn't live here putting refuse in the Resort's dumpsters, take down their license plate number and contact me immediately. I am offering a $10 reward for this information if it results in conviction and imprisonment of the guilty party. I will also throw in a lovely urn with lilies that you will be proud to display on your concrete slab.

Thank you, and have a pleasant day at the Resort!

Gretchen, Manager

PS There is a large dent in the bottom of the Coke machine, and a pool stick was found lodged in its can dispenser. Whoever is responsible for this act of vandalism must be turned over to me at once, or I will punish everyone in the Resort, including visiting family members.

The Coke Machine

The Resort has a Coke machine in the Clubhouse. Infrequently, the machine will actually dispense an ice cold soft drink when it senses that $1.50 in quarters has been deposited by an anxious and thirsty customer. The only problem is, the Coke machine is usually out of Cokes, which you don't realize until your sixth quarter has disappeared down the contraption's slot. By then it's too late. No matter how much you bang and kick the goddamn thing, or jam a pool cue up its can chute, you will not receive a Coke, nor will your coins be returned.

And if, by chance, the following day you politely mention to Gretchen that the Coke machine didn't have an Out of Order sign on it and that I lost $1.50 in it, in addition to the $45 it swindled from me on previous occasions, she will silently glare and sneer at me over the top of her glasses until the tips of your shoe laces melt and I feel sweat, or *something* really warm and unpleasant, trickling down your leg.

The Coke machine, even when it's working, sometimes regurgitates a Coke that has gone completely flat or is dispensed in a misshapen plastic bottle that looks like it was abused by a Canadian during a corn hole game. But don't waste your breath whining about this to Gretchen. She's got her hands full chasing down phantom Pit Bull shit slingers and Coke machine vandals. You'll get no sympathy (or refunds) from her, and you may have to devise other methods for retribution in order to receive any satisfaction at all.

Dog Playground

Like many RV parks that cater to canines, ours has a small fenced area where a Trailer Dog dog can be let off its leash to romp about, fetch sticks, and pick up dried turds left behind by other Trailer Dog dogs. With turd clenched firmly between his teeth, the proud Trailer Dog dog will prance and strut around the edge of the playground, hoping against hope that another Trailer Dog dog will happen by to admire the splendid turd the same way a politician gazes at the wrapper on a colleague's Cuban cigar. *That last analogy has no meaning now that the US and Cuba have reconciled. Thanks, Obama.*

Our Trailer Dog dogs' playground is equipped with an ornamental plastic doghouse and a cute little matching fire hydrant. It is, as the clever, hand-painted sign says, the "Doggie Comfort Station." Apparently, the sign itself has brought comfort to many Trailer Dog dogs who have visited the playground, as it is heavily coated with piss, and one corner has been gnawed off. The coordinating plastic doghouse is in much the same condition.

Other signs around the TD dog playground admonish guests to use the provided doggie poop bags to dispose of pet waste in the provided garbage can, or face blistering fines and the enduring wrath of "Management." Seeing as how neither poop bags nor a receptacle (for them) is actually on the premises, you can't really blame Trailer Dog dogs for risking Gretchen's fury by shitting and pissing on everything in sight. *I keep expecting her to put up a "No Dogs Allowed" sign next to the Doggie Comfort Station.*

There are almost as many piles of crap lying around the Doggie Playground as are lounging on hotel lobby couches at political conventions. And I wouldn't be at all surprised if some enterprising Trailer Dogs lob their Trailer Dog dogs' crap over the playground fence just to draw Gretchen's' attention away from damages sustained by the Coke machine. It's morally and socially unacceptable to do something that crude, of course, but you show me a Trailer Dog who gives two shits about morals and social decorum, and I'll show you someone who isn't a Trailer Dog and who hasn't met Gretchen.

Community Garden

The Resort's Community Garden was completed last summer, about 10 days before the average daily temperature started soaring to 112 degrees. The garden area, approximately 20 feet square, is comprised of 3 raised beds full of sand and desiccated, brownish material. The garden is cursed with full, unobstructed desert sun. Cactus can't even survive in it. Neither can weeds or the most ambitious green-thumbed Trailer Dog.

Right after the Community Garden opened, a single Trailer Dog, a tall, thin guy, with long black hair pinned up in a bun and Jesus-type sandals, showed up with 15 plastic tubs of seedlings. He dug and scraped and furrowed, and after a sweltering afternoon of industrious labor, leaned on his shovel and admired his own little slice of Eden - potential tomato vines, cucumbers, zucchini, lettuce, peppers, and whatever other vegetables grow in the middle of the Sahara desert.

That evening, Mr. Oyl, as we admiringly had begun to call him *because he looked like freakin' Olive Oyl* returned multiple times with water for his sprouts and seedlings. It was utterly exhausting to watch him struggle with the heavy buckets and the temperature still in the low hundreds, even from our gravity chaises under the hose mister and with a cold beer in each hand. We finally had to go inside, vowing never to subject ourselves to that kind of ordeal again.

It is impossible to know whether or not Mr. Oyl harvested anything other than sunburn and dehydration from the Community Garden. We didn't see him over there much afterwards, and a few weeks later he moved away from the Resort altogether. No one else has attempted to plant anything in the Community Garden, which is now being used as a refuge by javalina and rattlesnakes. It has also become a dumping ground for dog crap when the dumpsters are full. Gretchen recently threatened to hire a full time security guard to patrol the area and catch the culprits. I sure hope she doesn't go through with it.

Resort Reviews

Not long ago, just for the hell of it, I went online and entered the name of our Resort. The first 10 million or so hits led to porn sites. I didn't spend a lot of time perusing any of them, due to their outrageous prices and the fact that a lot of the same stuff is free on google images and on *Game of Thrones*.

Also, it's depressing to watch people doing things that you'll never get the opportunity to do unless your book sells a million copies and you can afford to hire a well-endowed blind man to service you. *No offense intended to the blind in the event Trailer Dogs is published in Braille at some point.* I did finally find mention of the Resort in unbiased reviews by folks who had stayed/lived here at one time or another. Many of them referred directly to Resort Management. Here are a few of the best ones:

We stayed there in a motor home for one week. The Resort was, for the most part, clean and well kept. But Jesus Christ on a spoon, the Manager of the place was a bitch from hell!!!! She screamed at me for letting our dog poop in the street, and we don't even HAVE a dog!!! She tried to fine us $250 for not cleaning up poop from a dog we don't have!!! This woman should be locked up!!! We will never stay there again when traveling. –**Hoosier Vagabonds**

The Manager of the RV Resort is definitely lacking people skills and may be certifiably insane. My wife was at the pool when an odd looking man with extra-large ears approached her and asked if she'd help him find his cock ring, which he said fell off in the pool. My wife was horrified, and immediately reported the incident. The Resort's female manager called my wife a "whore," and told her the two-piece bathing suit she had on was "inappropriate" for someone "…with tits the size and shape of camel humps." We packed up and left that afternoon. We were there in a 5th wheel. - **Travlin' Manny**

DON'T GO THERE!!! The Manager, Gretchen, is awful! She'd kill a zombie and eat *its* brains. We stayed in one of their rental trailers for two months, and nothing worked, not even the toilet. It was 97 degrees inside and the air conditioner was broken. Gretchen's husband, Lloyd, told us he would fix it while we were at lunch, but when we got back, he hadn't been there. The AC was still broken, and someone had stolen a bra and two pairs of my panties. I went to the office to complain, and Gretchen screamed at me for interrupting her. When my husband and I got back home in Ohio, we noticed that a $350 damage fee had been added to our credit card bill, along with a $100 fine for "negligent disposal of dog waste." Worst experience EVER!!! - ***Unhappy Trails***

CHAPTER 4

DOGS IN THE HOOD

Site 1: Gretchen & Lloyd Bird, & their dog, Charles "The Management"

Gretchen and Lloyd Bird, live in a 40-foot 5th wheel trailer with their Pekinese, Charles, whose muzzle is so flat, he might be part Fiorina Hound. *I apologize for that last remark. It was uncalled for, and I had no right to insult Charles Bird.*

Everybody hates the Birds. Even Charles has nothing but disdain for Gretchen and Lloyd, if he acknowledges them at all. This is rare in Trailer Dog packs, whose canine constituency generally admires its leaders, if for no other reason than they have opposing thumbs and can reach the handle on the refrigerator.

Every morning at 7:30, Lloyd carries Charles out to the Birds' patio, and places His Majesty upon a bed pillow set atop a lawn chair. From his lofty throne, Charles watches the parade of peasants pass by, livestock (other dogs) in tow. He doesn't pay much attention to the creatures who labor in his fiefdom, but the peons know Charles constantly makes mental notes of any rule infractions or misconduct. He will share his observations with Gretchen later on.

Charles is an unusual Trailer Dog dog, in that he simply won't be provoked into any type of undignified behavior. Neither bark nor growl passes his furry lips, no matter what situation may arise. Behind Charles' majestic air of authority, I sense there's a crotch-sniffing, ass-munching leg-humper itching to get out. But Charles is a regal, imperturbable soul, and besides, he has Lloyd Bird to perform those distasteful tasks in his behalf.

At around a quarter of eight, Gretchen and Lloyd emerge from their trailer to have a smoke and confer with Charles about any questionable behavior he may have witnessed. Charles doesn't have time for a lot of chit chat or pleasantries, however. As soon as he briefs them on the gathered intel and has issued the day's instructions, he demands to be carried back to his inner sanctum, where he will begin a series of naps that will see him through the day. Managing humans is exhausting business.

Lloyd Bird is a skinny, gnomish guy, with scrunched up features and big ears. Lloyd's ears, **according to Resort lore**, are the largest organs on the outside of his body. It's not clear what Lloyd actually does to earn his keep as co-manager of the Resort. At first I thought he was the groundskeeper. One time I watched as he picked up a few small limbs that had blown off a tree near his trailer, but then I saw him toss them into the empty bed of another resident's truck.

Oh, and there was the time I saw Lloyd use a pool skimmer net to scoop his hat out of the water, but I can't imagine that counts as pool maintenance work. Lloyd *is* very helpful to the professionals brought in to do electrical repairs or unclog a toilet in one of the Resort's rental units. You might even catch a glimpse of him and the repairman standing in the middle of the road while Lloyd skillfully points in the direction of the rental needing attention.

I'm not saying Lloyd's lazy. At spring break, when the snowbirds' college age granddaughters come to visit, he labors at the pool all day long, keeping an eye out for possible drowning victims, helping young women apply sunscreen, and retrieving the occasional dropped towel. In an emergency, Lloyd will jump in the pool with no regard for his own safety, to fish a bikini bra out of the water before it gets sucked into the filters. Despite his services, the nubile mermaids mostly ignore Lloyd, except to glance at one another, roll their eyes and make crude gestures behind his back. Even with the ingratitude and mockery, Lloyd perseveres.

Gretchen, whose perpetual scowl makes one think she may have fallen face first into a plate of rancid oysters, sits on her substantial ass all day in her air conditioned office. There, she keeps track of whose rent is overdue, composes warning notices about dog waste removal, and fleshes out ideas for cruel and unusual punishments. I've hinted at this elsewhere in **Trailer Dogs**, but Gretchen is very unsympathetic, and can be downright callous. Sometimes, even Lloyd seems to be a victim of her brutality, that is, unless Charles has learned how to make a fist and deliver a black eye.

Last year, I believe it was in early May, an elderly snowbird couple, the Vincents, left the park in their motor home and returned to Iowa. They had been coming to the Resort for the previous 10 years, and had pre-paid for and reserved their site for a whole year at a time. They had improved the site by putting a neat picket fence around the perimeter, and had purchased and assembled a decent size plastic storage shed in the back of the space.

The following October, I happened to be in the clubhouse, reading notices on the community bulletin board, when to my surprise, Gretchen picked up the office phone and actually took a call. Her door was ajar and I could hear her side of the conversation:

Is that right?

Well, she *did* look horrible when you were here, no doubt about it.

What do you expect *me* to do about that, Mr. Vincent? I know you paid for a year, but I could have rented that site out a hundred times just in the last month. It's a little too late to expect a refund, isn't it?

Well, I can't do anything about that either.

I can give you a week to pick it up - and the fence too. If you can't arrange it, I'll have no choice but to confiscate them for use elsewhere in the Resort.

Don't you take that tone with me, Mr. Vincent. These rules are in place for the good of everyone.

Good day to you, sir.

Gretchen came out of the office, sighing loudly and shaking her head. "Mr. Vincent thinks just because his wife died last month and he's not coming back to the Resort, that he's entitled to a partial refund. And can you believe he asked if I knew anybody who might like to buy that crappy plastic shed of his? Jesus Christ, the **nerve** of some people."

A few days later I was surprised to see the "crappy" plastic shed sitting beside Gretchen and Lloyd's trailer. They'd even fastened a little Halloween decoration to the side of it. And when the Community Garden was completed, guess whose picket fence defined its front border? The Vincents' welcome sign is now at the entrance. "The Vincents" has been painted out. Now the sign reads: "Welcome to our Friendship Garden."

The first thing Gretchen does when she gets to the office (which is less than 50 feet from her trailer) is take the phone off the hook. When a park resident calls to find out why the electricity has been shut off without warning, or why nothing's coming out of the water taps in their RV, all they get is a busy signal. If they could corner Gretchen long enough to ask her why all they got was a busy signal, she would reward them with a dismissive stare and say: "Because I was *busy*. Anything else?"

I know this is Gretchen's *modus operandi* because of the day I went to the office to discuss my mounting financial losses with the Coke machine and equipment in the laundry. After chewing my ass out for interrupting her office work and berating *me* for the machines' malfunctions, she commenced to rant about all the complaints she puts up with from everybody at the Resort. Pointing balefully to a waste basket overflowing with crumpled notes from the Suggestion Box mounted outside her office door, she seethed.

"Just look at this, would you? Nothing but gripes and complaints. Day in and day out. Sometimes I get so sick of all the whining, I pray the goddamn terrorists will carpet bomb this fucking park and burn it to the ground." When the tirade was finished, I decided it was neither the time nor place to mention that our cable TV connection wasn't working. Ducking my head and mumbling an apology for the interruption, I backed towards the door.

"Before you go," Gretchen said, her voice dripping with suspicion, "You wouldn't know anything about the dog shit that's been turning up on the corn hole court, would you?" I shook my head. "Well, keep an ear to the ground, and if you see or hear anything, be sure and let me know. Those fucking Canadians are threatening to form a grievance committee."

Site 23: Lonnie and Daisy May

From the day they check in at the Resort, Trailer Dogs are assigned a numbered space in which to park their RV. Assigning a site is not as easy as it sounds. A guest planning to stay a week might ask for the open site close to the pool, but someone else may have reserved it months ago and already put down a deposit. Gretchen has to make sure that the site is available on the day the person (who put down the deposit) arrives, or there ***will be conflict.***

Keeping track of reservations at RV parks is more complicated and tricky than hotel reservations, because guests arrive with their "houses" in tow. Some sites are too small to accommodate a 40+ foot motor home or trailer, and not all of the sites are "pull thrus," or open at both ends. Then there's the problem of backing a big rig into a space that already has other RVs parked on three sides.

Other factors may come into play, such as whether guests want to be near the clubhouse, whether they need full or partial hook ups to sewer and electricity, and how long they plan on staying. Long-term guests – guests who reserve a site for 3-12 months - get preferential treatment, of course, but not all sites are ideal for long-termers. Folks staying more than 3 months don't necessarily want to get stuck in an area of the park where overnighters come and go every day and interrupt their dinner to ask for help emptying their black water (shit) tank.

We moved to the Resort in January, smack-dab in the middle of snowbird season. Most everything in the park was already occupied or reserved. Gretchen didn't have a long-term site available at the time, so she put us in short-term-space, promising to assign a long-term spot as soon as one opened up, probably in two or three months when the snow in Wisconsin and North Dakota melted down to mid-rooftop, and the snowbirds could go home. When she called a few days later to say a long-term site had suddenly become available, we were thrilled.

Site 24, our new home base, was large, and near the end of a long row. Site 25 on one side of it was occupied by a Resort rental trailer, a moldy-looking affair at best, with a rotting wooden deck. On the other side, in Site 23, was an equally dilapidated 5th wheel trailer with a hand-built, ramshackle shed in back of it.

Whoever lived at Site 23 was using every inch of his allotted space and more. A utility trailer, loaded with junk and covered with a frayed canvas tarp, was parked toward the front of the 5th wheel. Miscellaneous items were sprinkled haphazardly around the trailer – half-dead potted plants, bits of lumber, empty buckets, and a small, chest-type freezer. Tree branches and limbs, cut into chunks and tossed onto a 4-foot high pile, were intruding on our new site.

Ecstatic at the prospect of having a permanent, shaded spot, my old man backed our 5th wheel into the site and leveled it up. Undeterred by the firewood leaning perilously toward one of our windows, he attached the sewer hose and connected us to the electrical box. We were home, even if we were living next door to Sanford & Son. Hopefully, Fred and Lamont didn't plan on lighting a bonfire any time soon.

For almost a week after we moved in, I caught only brief glimpses of Site 23's occupant. He wore black sunglasses with one earpiece broken off, a grubby red tee shirt, matching red baseball cap (so filthy the writing on it wasn't readable) and stained tan shorts. I didn't know his name, but I knew he had a fat black dog, named Daisy May. Every morning I'd hear him yelling "Daisy May, git on over here." It went on all day long:

Lord God, Daisy May, are you poopin' again?

Bark bark bark bark bark

What's that in your poop, Daisy May? Is that orange peel? Where did you get that orange, Daisy May?

Bark bark bark bark bark

What are you sniffin' Daisy May? Is that your own poop? Don't get in that, Daisy May!"

Bark bark bark bark bark

Sweet Mother of God, Daisy May, that's your third poop this mornin'.

Bark bark bark bark bark

Daisy May, you're steppin' in your own poop! It's all over the place. Jesus H. Christ!"

Bark bark bark bark bark

Good Lord, Daisy May, now you got orange poop on your foot.

Bark bark bark bark bark

Let's go home and git somethin' to eat, Daisy May.

Bark bark bark bark BARK!

Gretchen had been very explicit about the rules of the Resort, a central one being that ***dogs must be on a leash at all times***. Apparently Daisy May was not aware of this important statute when she walked up to me, off-leash and unattended, and inserted her cone-shaped snout in my ass.

"Daisy May, get on over here," I heard our neighbor yell from the vicinity of his trailer. But by then, Daisy May's head was too far up my ass for her to hear or respond. Her owner came around the front of our 5th wheel, leash in hand. "Daisy May, whatcha doin' there, girl?" he lovingly inquired.

It was perfectly obvious what Daisy May was "doing." I had an armful of clothes on hangers at the time, and could not fend her off from completing her extensive examination of my upper bowel. Our neighbor snapped the leash on her collar and pulled her back a step or two. It seemed that he had given us enough time to settle in, and now he was ready to pow wow.

"I'm Lonnie May and this here's my dog, Daisy," he said. "We live next door there in the fiver. That's my shed back there," he added, waving his hand toward the ratty old 5th wheel travel trailer and rundown shed in back as though I might not have noticed them before now.

Trying to be neighborly, I nodded and introduced myself, hoping like hell he'd go away so I could finish unpacking. It wasn't that I felt unkindly toward him. I'd been at it all morning and still had about 12 bins of clothing, dishes, and miscellaneous supplies to sort through and put away inside the trailer. My hopes for his swift departure were soon dashed.

"Now, see, you can't keep those boxes out here like that," he frowned, making note of the bins stacked on our patio. "Gretchen don't allow that. Why, she'll be on you like stink on shit," he said, releasing Daisy May's collar from the harsh restrictions imposed by her leash.

"Well, I'm just unloading them today…"

"And you better not let them dogs of yours bark' neither. You better be trainin' them against that."

As Lonnie continued to enlighten me about park rules, Daisy May wandered around our unpacked bins, sniffing curiously at each lid. Satisfied there was no food to be had in any of them, she redirected her attentions to the area near our picnic table, where she hunkered down and commenced to take a large crap.

Seemingly oblivious to his dog's breach of the very Resort rules he'd been citing, Lonnie went on…"Now, you need to keep leaves and shit off this patio," he told me. "Old Lloyd Bird ain't gonna do it. He don't do nothin' 'cept sit around the pool all day." Then, speaking in a tone of confidentiality, Lonnie added, "…And your old man's gonna need to climb up on the roof of your fiver and sweep that too. If he don't do it regular, that roof is going to turn to shit."

"Well, thanks for the tips," I told him, turning toward the door of our trailer, praying that his idiotic tutorial had come to an end. It had not.

"Hey, do urinal have a leaf blower?"

"Uh… your ***what in all***?"

"You know, one of them things you plug in and blow leaves off stuff? If urinal had one of them things, you could keep leaves and shit off your fiver real easy."

"No, we don't have a leaf blower," I said. "Maybe we'll buy one after we're all moved in."

"Well, hell…maybe I could borrow it off you some time. The roof on my fiver's really turned to shit."

I realized it was time to set a precedent about acceptable visiting hours. "Lonnie, it was nice to meet you, but I need to get back to work and get our things out of those bins."

"Yeah, you need to get them bins outa here pronto," he said authoritatively, "…or Gretchen's gonna be on you like stink on shit."

In the weeks and months following my first conversation with him, I found out more about Lonnie from other Resort Trailer Dogs, but mostly from himself and all that went on two feet from our window.

Lonnie keeps his shed double padlocked, and because he has a serious case of OCD, he comes out maybe 500 times a day to check that the locks haven't been tampered with. The shed is where he stores junk he gets from people moving out of the Resort, along with treasures he finds tossed by the side of the road, or in dumpsters.

When we moved to our new site, I gave Lonnie some things we no longer had any use for, and when he opened the shed to put them away, I got a glimpse of what's inside. It's crammed to the ceiling with box after box of the crappiest of crap, junkiest junk.

I tried not to notice the spider webs and packrat turds all over the floor. I didn't want to think about what might be hiding inside some of the moldy boxes. It's what nightmares are made of. I'd been embarrassed that some of the items I'd given him were a little on the tacky side, but in comparison with what he already had in his shed, they were pure gold.

On Saturday mornings, Lonnie gathers up his finest wares, loads them onto his utility trailer, and hauls them down to a deserted parking lot at the end of the road. There, he and his local compadres operate a weekend swap meet and trade center of sorts.

What it is Lonnie and his pals "swap" would be pure conjecture on my part, but for the next three or four days after the swap meet, Lonnie stays very close to home. When he does come out of his trailer, stumbling and with bloodshot eyes, it's to accompany Daisy May over to a neighbor's site so she can shit on their patio, or to make a quick run to the convenience store for beef jerky & dog food.

Lonnie is 62 years old and is a veteran Trailer Dog. In the year and a half we've lived here, I've never once seen him wearing anything other than the red hat and tee shirt and tan shorts. They might be the clothes he had on when he moved here twelve years ago. I'm never sure whether it's him or Daisy May giving off the funky dog smell. Neither of them bathes or gets bathed, or so it would seem. He said something about the shower in his trailer not working right, and even though he's lived here a dozen years, apparently he has never thought of using the showers in the clubhouse.

I doubt that much inside Lonnie's rundown old trailer is in working order. I know for a fact his refrigerator isn't, because one day I saw him dump a large bucket of frost in the street.

"Fuckin' fridge has to get defrosted ever six months." he complained, shaking his head ruefully. "Fuckin' thing freezes everthing I put in it."

"Ummmm…isn't that what a freezer's supposed to do - freeze?" Lonnie shook his head and looked at me with disgust, like I was the biggest dunce on the face of the earth. "This frost shit come out of the **bottom** part, not up in the goddamn freezer."

Lonnie bought his 5th wheel trailer used, with money he got from a settlement after an on-the-job accident he had in 2001 or 2002, working construction. The accident banged him up pretty bad. His legs are populated with big ropy scars and knots, and he walks with a pronounced limp. He says the pain gets bad and makes it hard to get to sleep sometimes.

I don't know exactly how Lonnie's accident happened, but whatever it was, the pinkie and ring fingers on his left hand are also missing. He's always talking about suing the doctors who patched him up after the accident, even though it was 15 years ago. He goes through the phonebook, leaving voice mails at the offices of lawyers he thinks might take his case on contingency, and gets furious when they don't call him back. He writes the lawyers' names down in case someday he wants to sue them for denying him his constitutional right to sue.

An incident that raised my suspicions about Lonnie being extremely accident prone happened the day I saw him spring forth from his trailer, holding a grayish towel over one eye. He leapt into his truck and roared off without even checking the locks on his shed, so I knew it had to be an extreme emergency.

When he returned in the late afternoon, Lonnie had a large patch over the eye, and was carrying a little white paper sack like the ones pharmacies put prescription medications in. A few days later the patch was gone, and the area around his left eye looked like raw hamburger meat. Standing next to Daisy May, he recounted what had happened.

"I got up like usual to feed Daisy May. I reached in the medicine cabinet and got my Visene drops and put 'em in my eye like usual. Only I got the fuckin' camphor oil instead! Fuckin' **camphor oil!**

"Man, that stuff stung like shit, didn't it Daisy May?"

"I mean, it 'bout burned my fuckin' eye out, didn't it Daisy May?"

"Daisy May, you was scared, wasn't you, girl?"

"You thought I done burned out my eyeball, didn't you, Daisy May?"

"Anyhow, I drove on down to the ER and they fixed me up with a patch and pain meds. Doc said if I hadn't got in there like I did, I wouldn't have me an eye no more. Dad wouldn't have no eye, would he, Daisy May?"

As he was telling the story, Daisy May wagged her stubby tail and looked up at him adoringly. She seemed very happy that Dad still had him two eyes. I noticed his dirty red tee shirt smelled faintly of camphor oil, but I didn't let on. It was a significant improvement over what it usually smelled like.

It's not clear whether Lonnie receives any type of disability, or if he has any source of income other than from odd jobs he does around the Resort and from the junk he sells out of the back of his truck. Whatever type of commerce he engages in, he apparently earns enough to pay the rent on his site, keep himself nourished with beef jerky, and buy 40 pound bags of dog food for Daisy May. Clothing and soap are definitely not regular expenses.

In his younger days, Lonnie may have looked a little like Glen Campbell. He has faint traces of the round-faced, rosy cheeked all-American boy Campbell was when he was in his prime. Nowadays, he looks like a man who was dragged 10 miles behind a horse, face first through cactus, and the horse was shitting in his path as it trotted along.

That doesn't stop Lonnie from thinking he's God's gift to women, though. One day a younger, attractive Latina, holding a plate wrapped in foil, knocked on his door. When he finally opened it, Lonnie reached out, grabbed the plate, and basically slammed the door in her face. She stood there a minute looking a little bewildered, then got into her car and drove slowly away.

"That Mex gal that was at my place yesterday is named Maria," he explained, even though I hadn't asked. "Her dad comes down to the swap meet and sells tamales and stuff. She was down there and got a look at me, and she's been chasin' after me ever since. Said she'd clean my trailer regular if I wanted her to, and bring me food. Then she went out and got herself a dog just like Daisy May. She probably thinks she's gonna get herself a rich American husband so she can stay over here legal, but I ain't gonna be havin' none of that wetback wife shit. She makes some good tamales, though, don't she, Daisy May?" ***Rich American husband. I looked for any sign of humor in his eyes. There was none.***

Daisy May is supposedly an Australian Heeler mix. What she's mixed with is known only to her biological mother. Her coat is short and mottled gray-black, and she has narrow, pig-like eyes. Her muzzle is shaped like a cone, and it reminds me of those cardboard horns they pass out on New Year's Eve.

While most of the other dogs in the Resort bark when their owners leave them alone inside their trailers, Daisy May only barks when Lonnie is around. I've concluded this is how they communicate with each other. Of the two, Daisy May is by far the easiest to understand. She smells a tad better too.

Daisy & Lonnie May

Site 102: Gerald & Lulu Karn

One afternoon as I was walking over by the Canadian section of the Resort near the corn hole court, an old trailer in a site across from the dumpster stopped me dead in my tracks. The trailer itself wasn't as bad as the site at which it was parked. A collection of sheep horns, cow skulls and deer antlers were scattered around one end, and odd bits and pieces of lumber littered the other end. Unfinished projects lay abandoned, with open paint cans and dried out brushes occupying most of the surface of the concrete pad. Two greasy charcoal grills, neither fit to cook on, were pushed to one side.

A small fence was "under construction" around the trailer. None of fence's sections were of the same height, or even made out of the same wood. On either side of the trailer's sagging wood steps were handrails, fashioned from different lengths of tree limbs. Some of them still had dried out leaves attached. Had the brothers Grimm lived in our times, this trailer and its creepy surroundings would have been the perfect setting for the cottage of an evil witch. If anything, it was far worse than Lonnie May's site.

Hanging from a wire next to the door of the trailer's only entrance, was a piece of wood cut in the shape of a bone. The bone had "Welcome" painted on it, at least that's what the artist was probably going for until he ran out of room after the "o."

The bone sign didn't seem very welco-ing, especially since on the other side of the door, a metal stand displayed a flag with a coiled snake on it. Underneath the snake were the words: "Don't tread on me." I stood there a minute, speculating what might happen if I knocked on the door. Would I be welco-ed, or would I be attacked by a big ugly snake?

Having made the decision to avoid treading on anyone, I was ready to move along, when I noticed a curly white head at the trailer's bedroom window. It was one of the cutest dog heads I'd ever seen. So cute, in fact, I thought for a minute it was a stuffed toy. Then it moved, and I could see a tiny pink ribbon in each of its ears.

The dog was smiling at me! I was transfixed. As I stood there trying to figure out how I could pull off a dognapping without triggering a snake attack, a woman walked up and stood beside me. She was also looking in the direction of the trailer. "Are you interested in Gerald's horns and antlers? He'll give you a good price. Not much call for 'em around here. Everbody hunts."

"Uh… no, we don't need any horns or antlers at the moment," I said. "I was just looking at that cute dog in the window."

"Oh, yeah - that's Lulu," the woman said. "She's one of them Bee-john Freezays." *Bichon Frise. I should have known - the happy, smiling face, the fluffy white fur. On my Bucket List of 500 or so dogs I wanted to own before I died, Bichons were in the top 20.*

"She *is* a friendly little critter," the woman laughed, "Gerald hauls her to the beauty parlor every few weeks, and he even cooks her food for her. Why, he treats that dog like she was his own kid!"

I backed away from the woman, crossing my hands in front of my throat to ward off a punch. A red pickup pulled up next to the trailer, and a man got out. Even though the weather was warm, he was wearing a ragged sweater and shirt buttoned to the collar. Stringy gray hair hung down from under a knitted beanie.

The man's face was expressionless, but he had a slightly crazy look about him. He retrieved something from the back of the truck, and as he walked toward the trailer, he tossed two more antlers on the pile. He glanced in our direction, quickly ducked his head and went inside the trailer without acknowledging our presence.

"Well, that's Gerald," the woman said. "He don't talk much, except about Lulu or his horns. Sometimes I don't think he's right in his head, if you know what I mean…" I nodded, thinking of Lonnie May. "I better get on back to the camper," the woman said, "We're in the Winnebago over there. We got three cats that needs baths, and their litter box ain't cleanin' itself." She chuckled as she turned and walked away.

Not long after the encounter with Gerald's cat lady neighbor, I was walking past his trailer just as Lulu was coming out the door. The white head with beribboned ears emerged first and looked around, surveying the weather. The head was followed by the fattest Bichon Frise body I had ever seen, bar none.

For a minute I thought the little dog might not be able to squeeze through the door, but she lumbered down the steps one by one, and paused at the bottom, panting heavily. When she saw me, she came waddling over, as fast as her short trotters would allow. Gerald was right behind her, his gray stringy hair poking out from the beanie. Up close, he reminded me of the guy who played Larry, the main brother to Darryl and his other brother, Darryl, on **The Bob Newhart Show**.

Little Lulu's enormous body was perfectly clipped, and not a grass stain marked her pristine white coat. I knelt down, and she tottered up and threw herself against me, nearly knocking me over in the process. The air around her smelled like the cosmetics counter at Nordstrom. *The dognapping was going to be even trickier than I'd first thought. I was probably going to need a sling or hoist of some kind to get her through that damn window.* As I crouched there, petting Lulu, Gerald stood close by, his face immobile and his eyes watchful.

"If you ever need a babysitter, I'm your man," I told him, as Lulu planted kisses on my face.

Gerald finally spoke. "I don't leave her much," he said "She gets too lonesome if I'm gone more than an hour or two. On Tuesdays I take her over to my mom's for her Bible study group. My mom's 93, and her and her old lady friends give Lulu too many treats and make a big fuss over her." *So that's why poor Lulu was morbidly obese, I thought. It's the Tuesday Bible study that's packing the pounds on her.*

"I seen you walk by here with your two dogs," Gerald said. "They's boys, ain't they?"

I confirmed his suspicions with a nod.

"I don't let no boy dogs git around my Lulu," Gerald continued. "She's been spaded, but you don't never know what can happen." I said my goodbyes and got up to leave. Lulu started to trot along behind me. Gerald came and herded her back toward his trailer. "Where abouts you live?" he asked.

"We're over in 24," I told him. "Next to Lonnie and Daisy May."

He seemed stunned. "Gretchen can't keep nobody in that site for long. That Lonnie May is off his rocker."

"How so?" I asked, thinking for some reason of pots calling kettles black.

"Well, for starters, his place ain't nothin' but a pig sty. He don't clean up nothin' He sells junk right out of his shed, and we ain't supposed to do that. It's against the rules. And I'll tell you what else. He don't treat his dog very good. He's all the time yellin' at her. And one day, *he yelled at my Lulu*."

Even though some of what Gerald said about Lonnie applied to Gerald himself, his assessment of our neighbor was spot-on, especially the pig sty part. The week before, after Lonnie mentioned that Daisy May had dug a hole in the middle of his mattress, I asked if he'd be interested in either of the two mattresses we had in storage. One was a futon that had never been slept on. It was inside a zippered nylon cover. We'd bought the other full-size mattress about 6 months before for a guest bedroom. Both were in great condition, clean, and stored inside heavy-duty plastic bags.

Lonnie, in his usual filthy tee shirt and shorts, mulled over the offer while Daisy May studied a pile of crap she'd just deposited in the middle of the street. "They're in pretty good shape, are they? How much are you wantin' for 'em?"

"If you want them, you can have them for free," I told him. "They're really nice - like new."

"Welp, I don't want no bedbugs crawlin' around in my fiver. Goodwill won't even take 'em if they been used." Lonnie said. His sudden fit of pickiness grated on me. Here was a guy who never showered, and who slept with a dog on a mattress with a hole dug in the middle.

"We're going over to our storage unit next weekend," I told him. "We'll pick up the mattresses and bring them here. If you want them, fine. If you don't, we'll just take them on to the dump. I don't give a shit either way." The following Sunday we brought the mattresses back to the trailer. Lonnie crawled onto the bed of our pick up to conduct a quality assurance inspection of them.

"They look pretty good," he confirmed, "But this futon ain't big enough, and they ain't comfortable anyhow. I don't want that one. This mattress ain't been slept on, has it?" I reiterated that it had been in a guest bedroom and only used a couple times when we had family visiting. "Well, I might take that mattress then. But I need to get my old one out first."

Later that afternoon, Lonnie maneuvered his old mattress to the door of his trailer, and my old man helped him pull it the rest of the way out. It was disgusting beyond belief. Dark stains covered every square inch of the wreck, and stuffing popped out of rips and tears on its grimy surface. And there, in the middle of the wretched hulk, was the gaping hole Daisy May had dug and nested in.

"I'm gonna need a little help gettin' that new one in here," Lonnie told us. After he'd helped Lonnie muscle the new mattress inside his trailer and onto the platform bed, my old man came back to our trailer and plopped down on his recliner. He was visibly shaken. "If only walls could puke…" he said, shuddering. ***"The Horror."***

We'd just settled in with a couple beers when Lonnie banged on the door. "You know, that new mattress don't fit," he said. "My fiver bed must be a queen after all." My old man froze. I could see the fear in his eyes. No way was he going back inside that trailer. "My old man's back went out helping you, Lonnie," I told him, "You'll have to put the old mattress back in your trailer by yourself."

"Oh ***hell***, no," Lonnie guffawed. "I'm for sure keepin' that new one even if it's too little. Daisy May's over there sleepin' on it right now. Anyhow, I already sold my old mattress to a buddy of mine." He turned to leave. "Hey, and I reckon I'll take that futon too. I got another buddy that wants to buy that one off me."

Gerald interrupted my train of thought, which had been a comparison of him and Lonnie. "You don't need any antlers or horns, do ya?" he asked. "I got some nice ones over there by my fiver, and I'll make you a good deal."

"Let me think it over and get back to you." I wondered briefly if he realized he was attempting to transact a private sale against Gretchen's rules. Lulu, bored with my attentions and miffed because there were no treats to be had, waddled off down the road.

"Lulu, git on back here," Gerald yelled after her. "Where the hell are you goin', girlie? Now, don't get into that. **LULU, GIT ON BACK HERE RIGHT THIS MINUTE.**"

All that was missing was bark bark bark bark bark.

Little Lulu & Gerald's Horns

Sites 45, 46, 47: The Lopp Girls: Virginia, Laurette & Claudia

The Lopp Girls aren't really "girls." I know Virginia is 82, because she told me so. Laurette has to be in her mid-60s, and Claudia is probably 5 or 6 years younger than Laurette. Still, I call them "the Lopp Girls" because it strikes me funny, and you know what I've said about writing what I want. If you want to call them something else, you'll have to write a book about them for yourself.

I'm not sure if all the girls share the same last name of Lopp, either. Virginia Lopp is a widow, and although her daughters, Laurette and Claudia, may have been married at some point in their lives, here in the Resort, they live separately and alone. Laurette and Claudia have twin park model trailers, and Virginia lives between them in a 30-foot travel trailer. Virginia bought the park models for Laurette and Claudia to keep them close by her, a fact she also told me.

Despite her 82 years and about 50 extra pounds, Virginia Lopp is a very attractive Trailer Dog woman. Her face is unlined and her skin is smooth. She keeps her silver hair in a neat, swept back style, and her clothes are always freshly ironed. I started to say I hope I look that good at 82, but hell, I wish I looked that good right now.

Virginia is outspoken, opinionated and assertive. She's a breast cancer survivor and has had a hip replacement, but she gets around fine, and is usually in attendance at Resort parties and functions, unless Gretchen, who she despises, is present. Oh, and one more thing. Virginia drinks like a fish. Well, actually more like an open ditch. She's never without a tumbler full of amber colored liquid. If you sit next to

Virginia at a meal and happen to sip from her glass thinking it's your iced tea, take it from somebody who knows: it ain't tea.

Virginia's trailer is fairly new, and her daughters are always out washing its windows or tidying up Virginia's site, which has a neat wooden deck built along the side. There's a tree next to the deck, and small painted birdhouses hang from every branch. The entrance holes in the little houses have been taped over so birds won't nest inside and mess them up.

Virginia enjoys sitting on her deck with the whiskey bottle tucked behind her ankles for the sake of decorum, and a glass with a couple ice cubes for the sake of a highball on the rocks. She watches everything that goes on in the park, and keeps track of who brings what to the potlucks. When a dinner or party is scheduled, Virginia always knows who makes the best chili and who she'll coerce into bringing pigs in a blanket.

Claudia is the youngest of The Lopp Girls. She has inherited Virginia's good looks, her assertiveness, her love of birdhouses, and her deep fondness for alcohol. Claudia is also the sister who's always cleaning something, whether it's Virginia's trailer or her own park model. If I ever passed by Claudia's and she wasn't dipping a scrub brush into a bucket of soapy water, I'd think I was in the wrong trailer park.

Claudia, like most Trailer Dogs, loves dogs. She has two, both of them Chihuahuas. Their names are Lucy and Dolly. Lucy and Dolly are identical, fawn-colored girls, and Claudia keeps them safe from predators behind a small fenced area, replete with comfortable little beds and a variety of toys that look as though they just came off the shelves at Petco. Incredibly, Lucy and Dolly are not yappers. Sedate Chihuahuas with the quiet, self-possessed demeanors of Golden Retrievers. It's unprecedented.

Chihuahuas are another of my Bucket List dogs, even though we've already had one, and I should probably stick with dogs I haven't owned before. But me and my old man were head-over-heels crazy about Cheekly, a black and tan Chihuahua we adopted from a rescue organization in 2006.

Horribly neglected, starved, and with a mouthful of rotten teeth, Cheekly weighed barely 5 pounds and was near death when he came to live with us. He'd been kept in a cage at a puppy mill and rarely let out for the first 5 years of his life. The pads on his little feet were as soft as marshmallows.

Cheekly was terrified to leave the house and didn't like to be walked on a leash, so rain or shine, we had to carry him out and stand beside him until he was ready to get down to business. We bought him a crate and left the door open, and for the first year he spent a lot of time in there whenever there was stormy weather, or sometimes when he was just too overwhelmed by a big, noisy world he'd never been allowed to explore.

It took months of trips to the vet and hands-on nurturing to rehabilitate Cheekly. Every day I brushed his few remaining snags and cooked custom meals for him (he was always ravenous). He slept in our bed with our other two dogs, and, as I liked to tell everybody, his ass was as smooth as the Blarney Stone from all the kissing it got.

Our efforts began to pay off as Cheekly started gaining weight and found his place in our motley pack. He joined the rest of the pack on trips in our small travel trailer, and he loved sitting on my lap in the truck or snoozing next to Ben as we sped down the highway.

Despite his tiny stature, Cheekly was the bravest dog we'd ever had. He was utterly fearless, chasing after dogs five times his size, and barking his lungs out when he saw someone he didn't know coming up the steps to the house. And that included ***everybody*** who ever came up those steps, because Cheekly couldn't see worth a damn, and many times he barked at his own reflection in the pane of the French doors.

We didn't realize the true extent of Ckeekly's visual impairment until the day he mistook a cow for a rabbit, and ran off in hot pursuit. When we finally caught up with Cheekly down in the pasture, he was patiently waiting for us, and the 1300-pound cow, in her infinite wisdom, was trying to hide behind a nearby tree.

One morning, about 7 years after we adopted him, Cheekly, for the first time ever, refused to eat his breakfast. We knew something terrible was wrong. Twenty minutes later he died in my arms of heart failure. The vet said that Chihuahuas usually lived longer, but years of neglected teeth, being kept in a cage and cruelly underfed, had finally caught up with our boy. I hoped that the years Cheekly was with us somehow made up a bit for his sad early life.

When Cheekly died, he weighed over seven pounds, and had been all over the country with us. He had found people who loved him, and other dogs he'd bonded with, and who had accepted him into their pack. It pains me to say this, but considering all of the rescued animals, wild and domesticated, physically abused, neglected or just abandoned, Cheekly was probably one of the lucky ones.

Cheekly had been beaten down by a life he didn't choose or deserve, and crippled by circumstances far beyond his control. He was a survivor of adversity - brave, adaptable, and willing to give his heart to humans he had no reason to trust. Cheekly the rescue Chihuahua, could, by anyone's definition, be regarded as King of the Trailer Dogs.

Three years after Cheekly's death, I thought I might be a little closer to getting over missing him so much, when I saw Lucy and Dolly peeking at me from behind the low fence at Claudia's. True to form, I immediately started thinking of ways to "acquire" the two Chihuahuas surreptitiously. My plot was quickly foiled, however, when I learned that Claudia was formerly in law enforcement, and it would be a piece of cake for her to track down her missing dogs and kick the shit out me.

Laurette Lopp is different in personality and in looks from her sister, Claudia, but you can tell she's related to Virginia because she's very plump and has similar features. Somehow, Laurette manages to look even more matronly than her 82-year old mother. Her salt & pepper hair is down to her shoulders and on the frizzy side. She wears men's shirts and pedal pushers, and big white sneakers that make her feet look as though she has on clown shoes. Laurette is the most tranquil of The Lopp Girls. While Virginia and Claudia will loudly dominate any conversation, Laurette stands quietly in the shadows, amused at their antics.

Regardless of Gretchen's rules about a limit of two pets per site, Laurette has three tiny, adorable Maltese-Poodles (Maltipoos). Winky, Blinky and Ned are named after the famous children's poem, Wynken, Blykin and Nod. The threesome are so irresistibly cute, it makes me understand why some mothers eat their young. They're boy dogs, and unlike Lucy and Dolly, they're yappers. I have to time my walks with our boys for when Winky, Blinky & Ned are inside with Laurette. Otherwise there would be a yap fest of epic proportions.

The reason Laurette escapes Gretchen's laws on the number of pets allowed at one site is because Virginia claims Ned is actually **her** dog, and that he "visits" Winky and Blinky from time to time. If there are people in this park that Gretchen will avoid conflict with at all costs, it's Virginia and Claudia. Virginia will just tell her to fuck off, but Claudia, with her background in law enforcement, could drop her in one swift move and perp walk her back to the office. It's a risk Gretchen is unwilling to take. It's rumored that Gretchen once sent Lloyd to do battle with Claudia over some dumb thing, and Claudia ended up grabbing him by the balls and daring him to say one more word. If Lloyd **did** say one more word, it was probably "uncle."

"She better never come 'round here threatenin' me and my girls," Virginia said of Gretchen one day when I stopped in for a chat and a "beverage." "I'll kick her ass up between her shoulders!"

"Nobody would know the difference, Mama" Claudia chimed in. "Her face already looks like a goddamn baboon's ass." This observation brought on snorts and hoots from everybody, except Laurette, who shook her head and blushed. "Oh, you two are just awful."

Laurette's park model, though it's the same exact make and age as Claudia's, is very different from her sister's. The most noticeable difference are the gee gaws - ceramic sunbursts, cherubs, plaques, decorative plates, etc., that all but obscure the exterior of the trailer-house. Families of plastic squirrels, frozen in place, climb over the tops of the windows and near the roofline. Strings of multi colored lights hang from hooks, and artificial vines dangle from pots attached to metal brackets. A fountain with water that changes colors is the centerpiece of the decorative splendor.

The area surrounding Laurette's trailer is even more crowded, with plastic flowers and whirly gigs of every shape and size. Several small tables are set up in the "yard," as though the Mad Hatter and March Hare are expected for tea, where they will be entertained by their hosts, 7 plaster dwarfs and (by actual count) 14 ceramic frogs in various sizes. The only thing missing from the scene is a partridge in a pear tree, and at Christmas, Laurette will add that to the tableau, next to a crèche with not one, but two Baby Jesuses.

Miraculously, it all works – at least for me, but I guess I'm not exactly a model for good taste. There's a certain charm to Laurette's neurotic clutter, and even though there aren't any small children living at the Resort, if there were, they too would be enchanted with her knack for knick knacks.

One day I told Laurette her yard reminded me of Disneyland, and she was so thrilled, I thought for a minute she was going to cry. Ever since then, when I walk by her place, providing I don't have our yappers along, Laurette invites me in to visit with Winky, Blinky and Ned. I could stay there all day playing with them, but I have to tamp down my craving for Malti-Poos when Laurette's around. See, Maltese and Poodles are **both** on my Bucket List.

Of the three Lopps, I'm most drawn to Virginia, and I'm not sure why. Maybe it's her good-hearted gruffness, or my sense that underneath the bravado, she's not as tough as she'd like everyone to think. Her greatest fear seems to be that something bad will happen to her "girls," and she's completely devoted to them even though they can obviously take care of themselves.

Claudia is retired from her career as a sheriff's deputy, and Laurette worked for years at one of those walk-in tax preparers, possibly H&R Block. Claudia and Laurette feel the same way about Virginia, and 99 percent of the time, one or the other of them is within shouting distance of her. Except for the day Claudia drove Laurette to town for a dentist appointment.

I happened to be walking by on my way to the laundry room, and Virginia, as usual, was sitting on her porch, nursing a whiskey. When she saw me, she rose from her seat and motioned for me to come on up.

"I got something I want you to see," she told me, "while my girls aren't around." I followed her inside her trailer, which was immaculate, thanks to the daughterly maid service it received. Virginia led me to the back of the trailer, and there on the bed, grooming its nether regions, sat a huge white cat.

My mother was a cat person, and throughout my childhood I competed (or felt I was competing) for her affections with a series of white, long-haired felines Mom referred to as "your little sister, Princess Snowflake," or "your little brother, Peter Cottonballs." Despite the affection I felt for my kitteh siblings, there was always lot of squabbling going on - tail pulling, face clawing, biting and malevolent hissing. Sometimes the cats even got in on it. *Joke alert, cat lovers. My cat sisters and brothers were actually very peace loving.* I was extremely suspicious that Mom loved her cat kids better than me. *Later, with the hindsight of an adult, I'm convinced of it.*

When the back of our sofa got scratched to ribbons, I got the blame. When a slimy hairball caused Mom to slip and fall in the bathroom, she was sure it came from my shower cap. And when shit clumps from the litter box showed up unexpectedly on top of the washer, I was always accused of "setting up" her precious darlings to take the fall. It was an egregious abuse of parental favoritism as far as I was concerned, and I resented it deeply.

One day I asked her straight out: "Mom, do you love Princess Snowflake better than me?" She scoffed. "Well of course not, dummy. I love Princess with all my heart and all my soul, and I love you just as much."

Now, the enormous white cat resting on Virginia's bed was giving me a bad case of PTSD. And it was about to get worse. "This here is Princess," she said. A pair of large, round green eyes looked up at the mention of her name. Then the Princess appeared to sigh, perhaps with boredom, and went back to her tongue bath. "She's gorgeous," I said, feeling a strange mix of déjà vu and jealousy.

"Well, Princess is 15, now. I don't know anything about cat years and all that, but it must make her about as old as me! Let's go fix ourselves a beverage," Virginia said, walking back to the front of the trailer, where two highball glasses were set on a table alongside a bottle of Bailey's Irish Cream.

"I need to ask you for a favor." Virginia filled her glass nearly to the brim and was about to the same with my glass when I stopped her. "Whoa there," I said, "I still have to get our clothes out of the dryer over at the laundry room. I don't want to end up with Lonnie May's drawers in my drawers."

"No danger there," Virginia chuckled. "That slob never washes his neck, let alone his drawers." Then she went on to explain what she wanted me to do for her.

"See, I ain't gettin' any younger, and all I got is my girls and that cat in there. And I love Princess as much as any human, and way more than some of 'em. When the girls' Daddy died in '85, he left me a little money, and I used it to pay off our house. It wasn't nothin' special, just an average tract house in southern California in an okay neighborhood. When I went to put it up for sale in '96, the damn real estate agent said it was worth over a million dollars! I about shit myself," she roared. "It was like I'd gone and won the lottery."

"Anyways, the girls and me come here, and I bought them their little houses and me this trailer, and here we all are, livin' the life of Riley. But we never go anywhere, what with the girls' dogs and Princess, mainly. We don't trust nobody to take care of them. They're our lives. For years now, I've been wantin' to take all of us over to Hawaii for a little vacation. It's on my Bucket List. We talked it over, and the girls said if I could get you to come by here every day and look in on our animals and keep 'em fed and watered, then we could go on our trip with some peace of mind. I'm prepared to offer you $500 to do that for us for a week, but it has to be done on the QT. Gretchen can't find out about Princess no matter what."

"Let me get this straight," I began, "You want me to come to each of your places every day, for one week, to feed and play with Winky, Blinky, Ned, Dolly, Lucy and Princess, for as long as I want, and you're going to pay me $500 for it?"

"That's the long and short of her," Virginia said, polishing off the Baileys left in her glass and pouring another. "And you don't have to do anything much with Princess 'cept empty her litter box and make sure she gets her Fancy Feast."

"Virginia, you've got yourself a deal," I said, "But only on one condition. You have to donate the $500 to my favorite animal rescue group." Virginia slapped the table in front of her. "Great idea! I'll write out the check right now, and tell the girls as soon as they get home."

So, that's how The Lopp Girls got to spend a week basking in the sun in Hawaii, and how I got to spend a week basking in the warmth of Poodle-Maltese-Chihuahua-Cat love. It was a win-win-win situation, and both Virginia and I got to check items off our Bucket Lists. The donation to the animal rescue organization was made in the name of Cheekly, The Bravest Chihuahua of Them All."

There was, unfortunately, a down side to the deal Virginia and I made that day. By the time I left her trailer, I was so trashed on Baileys that I forgot all about going to laundry room. When I finally got around to it late that afternoon, I was rewarded with still-damp towels piled on the counter.

A note on lined yellow paper scolded me at great length for being inconsiderate by not removing my wash from the dryer in a timely fashion, and threatened dire consequences, including eviction, if I transgressed again. Another, less comprehensive note on yellow paper, was taped to the dryer. It read simply: **Out of Order**.

Site 116: Ian Reeve & his wife, ?

There's something my Mom used to say that sticks in my head to this very day: *It's better to keep your mouth shut and appear dumb than to open it and remove all doubt.* I can't be sure, but it sounds like it might have been a direct quote from Helen Keller.

Another thing Mom constantly preached to me was: *If you don't have something nice to say about somebody, don't say anything at all.* But you know what? My Mom wasn't trying to write a best-selling, tell-all book, and as far as I know, she led a sheltered life and had never met a Canadian male.

If you know what you're doing, you can tell a Canadian male from an American male by reviewing his answers to these simple questions:

What is your name?
Answer: Gordon, Ian, Pierre, Niles, Heathcliff, Winthrop, etc.
(He's Canadian - they all have weird names like that.)

What is your Number One favorite sport?
Answer: Corn Hole
(He's Canadian)

What is your postal code?
Answer: wha..?

(He's American - he doesn't know that "postal code" is Canadian for "zip code.")

Now, I suppose some of the wise-asses among you readers are wondering: Why can't we save some time and just ask the guy where he's from? Well, that doesn't always work. Canadians are a secretive, duplicitous race. They like to blend in with their surroundings when they're in the US so they'll be mistaken for Americans. This is why very often you'll see a red and white flag with a big old maple leaf on it stuck in the ground in front of their rigs. They believe a familiar, everyday object - like a leaf on a flag - will throw you off their scent.

Other tricks Canadians employ to blend in with their American counterparts include speaking in loud, argumentative voices about politics, elbowing people aside at the buffet table, and scratching their privates in public areas, or as a Canadian would say: "Scratching me auld ball saque in Quebec." Hard to believe, but that's really how those people talk when they're back in their fatherland.

The main reason Canadians are so secretive about their nationality is so they can hoodwink unsuspecting Americans into betting on the outcome of corn hole games. It's disgraceful, I know, but it's the fastest way a Canadian can get his hands on good old American currency. Canadian money is worthless here in the States, but that doesn't stop Canuks from bargaining you down at a yard sale, and then trying to pay for your Grandpa's vintage truss with a five-shilling bill that has a picture of their king and queen on it.

Canadians, like Ted Cruz, come to the U.S. and take good Senate jobs away from Americans. This we know. They disguise themselves as

Americans and try to sabotage our elections so they can make us bow down to their goddamn king and queen, and accept free health care.

Other things you may not have known about Canadians is their refusal to drink American beer unless it's the only alcohol around, and as long as it's free. Even then, a Canadian will never drink beer from a can or a lady's boot. They're conceited and fault-finding, and they will ride an American until they wear out their spurs on his inflamed hind quarters.

Ian Reeve, the Canadian, and his old lady (whose name nobody knows even though she lives here with Ian in their gigantic motor home for six months out of the year) get very involved in Resort activities.

Ian is an indefatigable coordinator, who is constantly at the clubhouse, planning holiday parties, arranging group excursions to the golf course (miniature), and organizing corn hole matches. He is a short-ish, rotund guy, with a ruddy complexion and a red goatee with streaks of silver. He's usually dressed in freshly pressed khakis, a short sleeve shirt buttoned up to his chin, and Top-Sider deck shoes. In the eyes of a Trailer Dog, that shit plays like a three-piece Armani suit.

On the corn hole court, however, Ian transforms himself into a fireball of masculine pulchritude. Tank top drenched in sweat, fierce-eyed and beard glistening, Ian takes on all comers. His expertise in the sport is a dead giveaway of his nationality. For, if there's one thing that will expose a Canadian and reveal the naked truth about his heritage, it's an unmistakable gift for corn holing.

Incredibly, Ian gets along well with Gretchen. I think it's because he acts toady around her and offers to help her with chores, like making copies of new Resort rules and regulations, or having his wife clean the coffee urn in the clubhouse. Sometimes he even walks Charles for her, although he doesn't own a dog himself, and doesn't seem to be very fond of them.

When Gretchen was down with a migraine for a week, Ian thoughtfully had his wife make soup for her. Being even more helpful, Ian had his wife scrub the clubhouse rest rooms/showers, although keeping them clean is actually Lloyd Bird's responsibility. I imagine getting the rest rooms sanitized was quite a chore, as the time I was in the women's, it was filthy and had a fist-size hole in the wall across from the showers.

Ian and no-name hosted the last New Year's Eve party and Ian emceed it. For some reason, Gretchen and Lloyd Bird didn't attend. About 40 Trailer Dogs showed up, and after we had passed our food and beverage contributions to his wife, Ian directed us to assigned seats at various tables, and instructed us to remain seated until all the guests had arrived. A bit of a kerfuffle arose when the Lopp girls realized they had been assigned different tables, but Ian corrected the error when Virginia Lopp menaced him with a half-empty whisky bottle.

After all the guests had arrived and were ushered to their seats. Ian began to fill us in on the activities planned for that evening.

"Welcome to our annual New Year's Eve bash," he spoke into the mic. "We're going to have a blast tonight. First, I'm going to show you a few slides from last year's party, which I also hosted, and then I'll divide you into teams and we'll have game of Trivia, with prizes awarded. We'll play music later, and there'll be dancing. At my signal, you may all move to the refreshment table, where my lovely wife will distribute paper plates and cups."

Most of the party goers, who were already a little sloshed when they walked in the door, were chatting amiably with their neighbors and not paying much attention. Some had started to drift toward the refreshment table ahead of Ian's signal, and others were crowding around the makeshift bar. Ian was becoming increasingly agitated.

"Now, if I could just have your attention for a minute, folks…" The party goers remained oblivious. "***SIT DOWN AND SHUT UP!***" Ian screamed. The room fell as silent as the audience at a Martin O'Malley rally.

Then, from over at the Lopp table, Virginia's voice rang out. "***You*** shut up, you bossy little prick," she hollered. "No goddamn Canadian's gonna tell *us* how to run a party."

No one else spoke. Ian glanced around nervously. His wife seemed strangely pleased. After a minute or so, Virginia's raucous laughter broke the spell, and soon everybody joined in the merriment, including Ian.

The rest of the party went well, except for the trivia game Ian organized. Most all of the questions he'd prepared were about Canada - Canadian actors nobody had heard of, Canadian baseball teams nobody seemed to know about, Canadian beer, and, of course, corn hole rules, which nobody ***wanted*** to know about.

I was elected captain at my table, and my team members were all loaded to the gills and weren't contributing at all. One or two seemed to be passed out. But I'd seen Ian put a bottle of champagne with a ribbon on its neck in the fridge, and I was determined to win the Grand Prize, even if I had to cheat to do it. To that end, when a trivia question appeared on the projection screen, I'd pretend to write down a letter corresponding to one of the multiple choice answers.

Only one or two questions had anything to do with America, and both were kind of insulting. The first one was something about the Toronto Blue Jays winning the World Series, and the second asked who started the war in Vietnam. (a. Lyndon Johnson, b. Andrew Johnson, or c. Magic Johnson)

The second question triggered a violent reaction from one of my team members, Joe, a hulking dude with a shaved head, neck like a tree trunk, and a ring in one ear. As it happened, Joe was a Vietnam vet, and he apparently thought the question denigrated his service.

"That motherfucking hippy was hidin' out in Canada and dodgin' the draft while I was over in The Nam, killin' gooks and fightin' for his fuckin' freedoms," he raged. "I ought go over there and stomp his goddamn brains out."

It wasn't any use explaining to Joe that Ian was a Canadian citizen during the Vietnam war, and therefore not eligible for the American draft. I reached out and patted his massive arm, hoping to calm him down before a fight broke out.

"Don't waste your breath, Joe," I told him. "In about 20 minutes we're going to light up that dick's wine cellar and put out the fire with a bottle of champagne."

When Ian read the answers to the trivia questions aloud, I wrote down the correct number on our team scorecard. Each team captain totaled his or her team's score, and my team got one question wrong, because I hadn't thought it would be as believable if we got 100% correct.

None of the other teams seemed to care about the outcome. In fact, most of them were over grazing at the refreshment table, or outside, vomiting in the parking lot. Ian motioned for me to come up to the front of the room. He put his hand over the mic and leaned in close to my ear.

"Look, I know you cheated on the trivia answers," he whispered. "I saw you. The right thing to do here would be for your team to forfeit the game."

I was flabbergasted. I'd saved that sniveling, draft-dodging, little corn holer from a good ass-whuppin', and now he had the gall to accuse me, a natural born American patriot, with cheating on his lousy trivia game? I directed Ian's attention to Joe, who was squeezing his whiskey bottle and glaring menacingly in Ian's direction.

"See GI Joe over there in the camouflage jacket? He engineered the whole thing, Ian. It was his idea of a joke, and now he wants his champagne. But if you want to go over there and call him a cheater, be my guest."

Ian studied Joe for a minute, shifting nervously from one foot to the other. "Well, it sounds like you didn't have much choice then," he conceded, handing over the frosty, beribboned bottle. "Congratulations."

"No, I didn't have a choice, Ian. But the good news is, Joe's been asking about your corn hole games. He's interested in putting together an American corn hole team here at the Resort."

Ian's face it up like a million bucks. "You don't say? Really? Why, that would be fantastic! I'll go over and talk to him aboot it tomorrow. Gretchen would kill me if she knew I told you this, but a long-term site's going to be opening up in the Resort next week. It might be a chance for you to get away from Lonnie May and that horrible dog of his."

I took the champagne back to our table. By then, most of my teammates were either passed out, or slow dancing on top of the billiards table. After giving Joe a healthy swig from the bottle, I drank the rest of it all by myself. In spite of all our troubles, it was shaping up to be a pretty good year after all.

I waited a few days after the New Year's Eve party before I went to Gretchen's office to ask about the long-term site opening Ian had mentioned. "And just how did you find out about that?" she asked, peering at me over her half-glasses.

"I think somebody at the New Year's party mentioned it," I told her. "Whoever it was said if we wanted it, we should put dibs on it right away."

Gretchen laid aside some files she'd been working on and looked at me with suspicion. "Why do you want to move from the site you're at now? Has Lonnie May been up to something I should know about?"

"No, well, not exactly…." I fumbled for an answer that wouldn't make me out to be the rat I had become.

"He isn't getting drunk with his buddies and shooting his pellet gun at the dumpster again is he?"

"Oh no, nothing like that," I lied.

"Well, I know for a fact he's not cleaning up after Daisy May," Gretchen grumbled. "People have reported to me that she craps all over the place, and he's not disposing of it properly. I've already written him up twice over it. He owes me five hundred dollars in fines, and he's always late on his rent. I've got just about enough ammunition to evict him and that mangy dog of his from the Resort as it is."

"Where would he go?" I wondered aloud, "He doesn't have a pot to piss in, his legs are a mess, and his old truck couldn't pull that 5th wheel 10 feet."

"That's not *my* problem," Gretchen said sharply. "He's a no good bum and everybody knows it. I don't care if he ends up on the street, selling pencils out of a tin cup. We've got too many losers here as it is. If you want the site, you'll have to pay at least three months' rent in advance. There are people calling every day wanting to make reservations for long-term sites."

"Where is the site exactly?" I asked

Gretchen had already gone back to thumbing through her papers. She didn't even look up. "It's not far from the corn hole court," she said distractedly. "A couple in a Winnebago are there right now, but they'll be leaving in another week."

Oh, wow…she was talking about the cat lady's site. We'd be neighbors with Gerald and his horn collection. "I thought the people in the Winnebago lived here year round?"

Gretchen sniffed. "They did. For three years. But right before Christmas, I told them if they didn't get rid of one of their cats, they'd have to leave the park. They have *three* of the damn things, and they walk them on leashes. Can you believe that? Cats on leashes! Poor Charles gets upset every time he sees them. They put up a fuss, but rules are rules, and I decided we can only allow 2 pets to a site. So, they're moving, ***thank God***," she sighed with exaggerated relief. "Do you want that site or not?"

We had discussed it at length, and had decided we really wanted to get away from Lonnie and his aggravating weirdness - the sooner the better. But something in Gretchen's crack about "losers" stuck in my craw.

Gretchen wasn't any smarter or any more entitled than the rest of us, and she used her position as Resort Manager to reward or punish as she saw fit. She demanded respect and obedience from people she derided as "losers" - people whose rent paid her salary while she made up the rules and enforced them on a whim. Hell, when you got right down to it, she was no better than most of the people in Congress.

"I don't think we want that site after all, Gretchen. It's too close to the corn hole court and that dumpster that always smells so bad. Say, Ian and his wife live over there, don't they?"

At the mention of Ian, Gretchen snapped to attention and leveled her steely gaze on me again. "I just remembered that Ian was the one who told me the site was going to be available," I said as I walked out the door. "But don't say anything. He'll kill me if he finds out I told you."

Site 57: Cripple Jon

Before you start wagging your head and getting all politically correct about my referring to him as "Cripple Jon," let me clue you in. First of all, Jon isn't a cripple, he's a paraplegic. And his name isn't Jon, either. Jon has been in a wheelchair since he was 22, broke up with his a girlfriend, got drunk, and drove his Mustang off a cliff somewhere in Nevada.

Jon wasn't trying to kill himself over the breakup or anything like that. In fact, he says he had a hooker with him when the car went off the cliff. When he tells the story, Jon never says what happened to the woman. I have reason to suspect she may have been killed in the accident, and that Jon emphasizes the fact that she was a prostitute because he stupidly thinks it'll ease everyone's mind about him being responsible for her death.

Jon will also tell you that being paralyzed at 22 ruins a man's life, even if his parents sell their house, pay all his hospital bills, and give him round-the-clock nursing care right up until they die.

Jon's folks scrimped and saved and managed to put aside enough money to buy him a park model trailer, a car equipped with hand-operated brakes, and enough cash to live on for the rest of his life. He's 44 now, and according to him, this was the **_very least_** they could do for him. They never should have bought him that Mustang, he says resentfully. If they'd just got him a Volvo or a Datsun, why, he might still be walking on his own today.

Nobody feels sorrier for Jon than Jon does for himself. When he's rolling around the Resort in his wheelchair, he'll corner you to fill you in on his latest bladder infection or bowel problem, and how he'd love to get a good job if only all the goddamn "wetbacks" weren't making it impossible to compete.

Whether it's a result of his paralysis, or whether he's had a speech impediment his whole life, Jon is sometimes difficult to understand, even when he's yelling. "Thoth fucking beanerths get all the bethst knobs," he'll rant about Mexican immigrants. "I wath in El Patho one time, and my aunt took me down and thowed me where they thwim acwoth the wivver to get to the Unina Thtates."

Jon says he's willing to do almost any kind of work, but would prefer an executive position, something that isn't too physical, and which doesn't require him to be present all the time, in case he doesn't feel like getting out of bed that day. What he'd really like to do is work in a call center, because Jon likes to talk on the phone - a lot. It would be nice to work in an air conditioned building, have his own office or cubicle, and be able to share his opinions on immigration with the folks on his call list.

"Lash mumph I went to a interview for a call thinner job," he told me. "Thoth ath holth din hire me cauth I can't thpeak Mexican. They dithcriminate against you if you don't thpeak Mex. Mexthus get all the breaks."

I wondered what it would be like to receive a telemarketing call from Jon, telling me I'd won five hunner dollarth and three dayth in Loth Vegath…but first I'd have to attend…a thympothiun about time thares. I also wondered what Jon would do if he worked at a call center and was given a list of people with Mexican surnames, like Rodriguez or Garcia to contact? I guess it wouldn't matter much. As it is, Jon is incomprehensible in English, and, as he frequently points out, doesn't "talk a lick of Mexthican."

Some days Jon will roll right by without so much as a nod or wave. He can be ice cold and unfriendly unless he's in the mood to complain about his physical predicament or get into an idiotic rant about how immigrants are ruining America.

Like Lonnie, Jon must have some rough nights with pain that keeping him from sleeping well, and I suppose it's natural for him to want to blame his misery on anybody and anything but himself. One thing I've for sure noticed is that if somebody holds a door open for him or picks up something he dropped while he was traversing the Resort in his wheel chair, Jon gets downright snippy with them. "I don't need you to do that for me," or "I can do that for mythelf." he'll grumble at the would-be Samaritan.

When he's in a lighter mood, Jon will stop and pet our boys and make over them. He thinks Sully looks like the Toto dog in **Gone with the Wind**. I have a feeling he got **The Wizard of Oz** mixed up with **Gone With the Wind**, maybe because both have something to do with wind, although "wind" is in the title of one, and in the form of a tornado in the other. Sully *does* kind of look like Toto, though.

Jon says Ben is too pretty to be a boy dog, and he's right on that too. Everybody refers to Ben as "she," even after they find out his name is Ben. Every time they see Jon coming toward us, Ben and Sully try to run the other way to avoid him. I think they're afraid of the wheelchair. Once they see who's in it, though, they both try to jump in his lap. I haven't told Jon that Sully's part Schnauzer and part Mexican

Chihuahua. I'm afraid he might start calling him a "Beaner" dog. I've got it in my head that if Jon got himself a companion dog, he'd be a lot happier. Maybe I'll suggest that to him sometime.

Cripple Jon Update

This is interesting. I suppose I could have left it until the end of the book, and in fact, I had already moved on to writing about other Trailer Dogs, when my old man passed along the information. But I thought I should write about it while the image of Cripple Jon is still fresh in your mind.

We hadn't seen Jon in several weeks, but yesterday when my old man was out walking the boys, he came rolling down the street, headed in their direction. He was not alone. A younger, attractive, dark-haired woman was pushing his wheelchair, and Jon had hold of a leash, at the end of which was a black dog that my old man at first thought was Daisy May because of its cone-shaped muzzle.

Upon seeing the wheelchair and the strange dog, the boys commenced raising hell, so my old man took them through an empty site and led them back toward home. He said Jon was smiling, and that his companion seemed very attentive. Clearly ***something*** was going on between them.

The scenario sounded vaguely familiar, especially the black dog with the cone-shaped muzzle that looked like Daisy May. Then it hit me. The woman ***had*** to be Maria, the Latina who brought Lonnie tamales and had a dog like Daisy May. Maria may have found herself an American husband after all. And Cripple Jon may have found he likes hot tamales better than he thought he did.

Site 62: Marv & Patty Greer

Marv and Patty are snowbirds from Wisconsin. The Greers leave their 34-foot 5th wheel trailer parked at the Resort year-round. Gretchen only charges them half the regular site rate when they're not here using the facilities, and sometimes she rents out the other half of their site to short-term guests who need a place to park their ATVs or other "toys" they bring along on vacation.

I'm not sure if people who store their RVs at the resort are aware of Gretchen's off-season parking "arrangements" at their sites, but even if they disapproved they wouldn't say anything to her, because she'd just tell them to haul their goddamn RV back to Madison or Timbuktu, or wherever the hell they were from. Us Trailer Dogs will put up with almost anything, even verbal abuse from the Queen of Mean, to save a buck or two. Been there, done that, as they say.

Patty and Marv Greer are not the usual breed of Trailer Dog, in that they don't have dogs or cats, and they dress a lot nicer than the rest of us even when they're just farting around their rig. But by Trailer Dog standards, they're ultra-weird. When we first moved to the Resort, their brand new 5th wheel was parked in the site directly behind ours, and we saw them to nod and exchange small talk pretty much every day.

One weekend we were shopping at Walmart when I saw Patty approaching me from the end of the aisle. She walked right up to my cart, and with a blank look on her face, said: "Excuse me, but do you know where the chicken bouillon cubes are in this store? We're from

Wisconsin, and they're in a different place in our Walmart." Marv was next to Patty when she asked me about the bouillon cubes. He didn't say anything, but just stood idly by his wife's side, grinning like a half-wit.

"I think they're over a couple aisles," I said. "Tell you what. I'm headed that way. I'll pick up a jar for you and bring them over later." Patty gave me a funny look, thanked me, and walked away, Marv tagging along behind her like a faithful old dog. I bought the bouillon cubes, and that evening my old man took them over and gave them to Patty, who was completely taken by surprise.

Later, she knocked on our door and I stepped outside. "I'm absolutely mortified." she began. "I didn't recognize you in Walmart because you were all dressed up and had makeup on, and you looked attractive - like somebody who knew what she was doing - and well, I just didn't realize it was *you*. Then I waited at the checkout stand for you to bring the bouillon, but you didn't show up, so I didn't know what to do or think."

It seemed to me that Patty wasn't capable of thinking, period, but she sure knew how to lay on a back-handed compliment. She also didn't know when to shut the hell up.

"I thought you might have been one of those crazy women who shop at Walmart," she laughed. "But then when your husband came over a minute ago with the bouillon cubes, I made the connection right away. It was like a light came on in my brain." **More like a flickering candle in an empty closet, I thought to myself.**

"What do I owe you for the bouillon cubes?" she asked, clearly not aware that she'd just insulted the shit of me. *If there's one thing I live in fear of, it's somebody taking a picture of me on their phone while I'm shopping at Walmart and posting it on the internet. Believe me, it could happen.*

"Not a thing, Patty. Consider the cubes a gift from me to you," I said, wanting to get rid of her as soon as possible. In the background I could hear my old man trying to suppress laughter. Unable to do two things at the same time, he failed to suppress an extremely loud fart. "That was Sully." I told Patty. "He probably doesn't recognize your smell."

Several months after the Walmart mix-up, Patty and Marv were getting ready to go back to Wisconsin for the summer. A few days beforehand, Patty asked if I'd help her load some of their stuff into their truck. They were leaving their 5th wheel behind at the site. Both she and Marv have undergone multiple back surgeries without very good results, and seeing as how I was eager to see them go, I agreed to do it, hoping to prevent any last minute postponement of their departure due to health issues.

Patty sat at their site's picnic table and carried on a one-sided conversation as I lifted the heavy bins onto the truck bed. She went into a rap about their middle-aged son, Todd, an only child, and how irresponsible Todd was, and how they loaned Todd money and Todd never paid it back, and how Todd was twice-divorced and couldn't hold a job, and how, although he was a free spender himself, Todd was extremely critical of how his parents spent *their* money, because, after all, what if they up and died and Todd couldn't afford to bury them if they'd gone and spent all his inheritance? To hear Patty tell it, she and Marv might end up as practice cadavers at some medical research center. Personally, I thought that would be an excellent use of their remains.

When she finished grousing about Todd, Patty started in on Marv. "You know, I just hate his guts," she confided without missing a beat. "I don't even know how it happened. We've been married for 48 years, and now I can hardly stand to look at the man. One day I just told him, 'Marv, I'm not doing the cooking anymore.' He said ok, that he would fix our dinner most nights, and I told him, 'No, I'm not cooking, period. If you want to eat anything at any time, you'll have to fix it yourself.'"

Patty paused for a breath. "And then I told him a few other things I wasn't going to do anymore, like laundry and housework. I said, 'Marv, if you want your clothes washed or the toilet scrubbed, you're going to have to do it.' And he has. But I still hate him, and I'm mean to him and I don't know why. He's been good to me and I get anything I want, but I just can't stand to be around him. That's why we got this big trailer with two beds. Sometimes I hate him so much I make him go sit outside, even when it's raining."

That explained why on rainy days I often saw Marv sitting forlornly in their truck.

"Lately, I've been thinking of ways to kill him," Patty went on. "But everything I come up with ends up with me going to prison. Sometimes I think it might be worth it."

"Do you ever have dreams where you're ripping the skin off Marv's face with your bare teeth?" I interjected.

Patty froze. "Oh, God yes! I just had one of those last night, in fact! I was ripping the flesh off Marv's cheeks with my bare teeth. I have that dream all the time. Do you have dreams like that about your husband too?"

I locked eyes with her. "Of course not," I lied. "That's some pretty sick stuff, Patty. Have you thought of seeing a shrink about your feelings?"

Patty stepped back and looked confused. "Well, no…I…I would never act on something…"

"You should see a psychiatrist as soon as you get back to Wisconsin," I told her bluntly. "This doesn't sound good at all. In fact, I think I saw something on Oprah about early onset dementia that can be caught from using a hot tub that old people peed in. You need to get checked out right away. Does Marv have any idea that you feel this way - that you actually daydream about doing him in?"

"Not really… although one time he joked that I might be trying to kill him for his life insurance. I told him he was just being paranoid."

The day after Marv and Patty left for Wisconsin, I was out walking the boys. We came around the corner, and there was Lonnie, pissing on the side of his trailer. His "flow" seemed pretty substantial for a guy his age, but as we came closer, I realized he had a hose in his hand, and was washing off the side of his trailer. "Fuckin' birds," he muttered when I stopped to say hi.

"How's Daisy May doing?" I asked. "I haven't seen her in a day or two."

"She either ate somethin' bad over by the dumpster or the goverment's been sprayin' poison out of them jet contrails again. She's fine now. She's in there, lookin' out the window to see what your little shit's up to," he said, gesturing toward Sully with the hose.

Sully jumped back as the water splashed near him. I looked up at the dark window, but couldn't see anything. If Daisy May was there, she was invisible. Sully was growling softly at my side, but his censure was aimed at Lonnie, not Daisy May, for the near dousing.

"The Resort is emptying out fast," I said, "Patty and Marv left yesterday."

Lonnie turned off the hose. "Yeah, and I'm glad they did. Marv's ok, but that Patty's a crazy old bitch. I think she was the one complainin' on me to Gretchen for lettin' Daisy May shit on their site."

"You're probably right," I agreed. "It sounds like something that crazy old bitch would pull."

Site 11: Phyllis and Bill Crane

The couple at the end of our row (Tulip Street), are Phyllis and Bill Crane. Bill served in the Marines, even though he hasn't killed anybody (to my knowledge) or been in a barroom brawl (again, to my knowledge) since the mid-1960s.

The Cranes have a manufactured park model, and in my opinion, they have the best site and the best house in the park. It's a one-bedroom, with a small living area and kitchen with a dining table and residential size appliances. It has actual closets and walls that you can hang actual pictures on. Best of all, it has an actual bath tub that you can take an actual bath in, with actual bath salts, and actual hot water that comes from a 10-gallon hot water heater.

Bill and Phyllis's other home is in Montana, where at one time Bill ran a remote, 1600-hundred acre cattle ranch and Phyllis taught school for several years before they started a family. According to Phyllis, it was a hard life and a lonely one, what with their ranch being 50 miles from the nearest town. She spoke of winters so harsh that she was often scared out of her wits when Bill had to go out to the barn in the middle of a blinding snowstorm, and could barely find his way back to the house 300 feet away.

Still, the Cranes managed to raise four children there, and gave each of them a college education by selling off parcels of their acreage. They remain close to their kids, even though none of them stayed in Montana. Two live in the northeast, one is a Floridian, and the fourth lives in the Chicago area. They have six grandchildren, and Phyllis, loving children as she does, wishes they lived next door to her. There's lots of visiting back and forth all year long. In mid-April, Phyllis and Bill pack up their stuff in an enclosed trailer and head back to Montana, where they remain until late October, when they come back to the Resort for the winter.

Phyllis is an enthusiastic gardener, and she's turned their site into a miniature Garden of Eden. Flowering shrubs surround the covered patio, and potted plants line the front of the small deck Bill built along the side of their park model. Phyllis even created a "secret garden," tucked behind the shrubs and vines, replete with a stone bench, more potted plants, and a small, gurgling fountain. It's a shaded haven in hot weather.

As soon as they get back here from Montana, Phyllis starts making the rounds at nursery centers to buy plants and other garden supplies. There are other green thumbs living at the Resort, but none as dedicated and capable as Phyllis. Her geraniums alone grow to the size of giant Sequoias, and their trunks can be driven through in a golf cart, providing one has had enough weed and booze to imagine one has accomplished such a thing.

I met Phyllis and Bill one morning as I was walking the boys. Phyllis was trimming back the vines around the secret garden, and was wearing a spotless flowered jacket that looked like it just came off the hanger, white gardening gloves, and a wide-brimmed straw hat. I judged her to be in her mid-to late seventies. She was also wearing red lipstick and full makeup. Phyllis is one of those women who can make you feel like one of Cinderella's ugly, dumpy sisters, and if she wasn't so damn nice, you might want to smack her for it.

When we stopped beside the patio, Phyllis knelt down and greeted the boys, first Ben, who put his paws on one of her knees and gave her a slurpy kiss, and then Sully, who, not trusting the intentions of the straw hat, backed up and growled. "Oh, look – he's afraid of my hat," Phyllis said, removing it to reveal a short bob with silver highlights. Sully, satisfied that no skullduggery was afoot, stepped forward to receive his honors and tributes. Phyllis was effusive, and he was not disappointed.

A voice from the shadows of the vine-covered patio boomed. "Come over here and have a seat." It was Bill, Phyllis's husband. Without thinking, I obeyed him. Amazingly, Ben and Sully followed suit, sitting down quietly at my feet. Phyllis sprinted up the wood steps of the park model and disappeared inside. "Mother's getting refreshments," Bill informed me. "Oh, I can't really stay…" I said, rising from my seat.

"Sit" was all Bill said. And I sat. He was old, but like Phyllis, he was still nice-looking and robust, with a military bearing. His voice had that certain authority that caused you do whatever the hell he told you to, and do it fast. That, I soon learned, was the result of his years as a "Top Kick" in the Marines.

Bill leaned toward me. "What do you think of that goddamn Gretchen and her goddamn moron husband? What a pair of fucks." Startled by the sudden string of curses from a guy I didn't even know, I wasn't sure how to respond. "They're something else." was all I could think of to say.

"You got that right," Bill said. "I told that asshole Lloyd if I ever catch him hanging around my granddaughters when they visit, I'm going to cut off his goddamn balls and gut him where he stands."

"You would be within your rights," I agreed. At that moment Phyllis appeared at the sliding door with a tray holding a pitcher of iced tea and three glasses. Bill rocketed out of his chair and ran to help her. "Let me get that for you, Mother," he said solicitously, taking the tray from her. "You go sit down and I'll fetch the cookies."

"Thank you, sweetie," Phyllis said with a smile. "And could you please get the napkins and coasters while you're in there?" Phyllis filled our glasses with tea, and Bill offered the plate of cookies. I'd been trying to cut down on sugar, and started to politely decline. Sensing my hesitation, Bill pushed the plate under my nose. "Take one." To be on the safe side, I took two.

"Now, what were you two chatting about while I was in the house?" Phyllis asked.

"I was just telling our neighbor about The Duke," Bill fibbed, offering me another cookie, which I respectfully accepted.

"Oh, yes, our Duke," Phyllis said, a melancholy look clouding her face. "Duke was our Border Collie. Lived to 18-can you imagine? Duke was the smartest, sweetest dog we ever had. He worked cattle on the ranch his whole life. Slept out in the barn and refused to set foot in the house, no matter what the weather was. He knew every trick in the book and then some. Bill trained him from time he was a puppy. He even learned hand signals. Bill and Duke were inseparable, weren't you, dear?"

"That we were, Mother, that we were," Bill said wistfully. He appeared to brush a tear from his eye, then sprang once again from his chair. "I'll get us some more of those cookies, Mother," he said. Tapping the arm of his empty seat, Phyllis smiled sweetly. "Sit, Bill," she said, Bill sank back down in his seat, looking a little contrite.

Marines claim they "fear only God." Based on what I've witnessed time and again with the Cranes, at least one Marine, Master Sergeant Bill Crane, fears only his wife, Phyllis.

Over the next few months as I came to know her better, I admired Phyllis more and more. She was smart, interesting and one of the most competent, best-organized people I'd ever met. She traveled a lot, was well-read, and had been to almost every foreign country you could name. She was also generous with her time, and loved to entertain on their patio. She never asked a guest to bring anything – the Cranes provided all the food and beverages, and afterwards, she and Bill did the clean up by themselves. They made quite a team, with Phyllis serving as Commanding Officer.

The Cranes' patio was forever undergoing redecoration. Bill, move those 12 geranium pots back to the other side. They don't look as good on this side of the patio as I thought they would. Bill would grab a couple of the geraniums and hustle them to the other side without a single complaint or a "goddamn" crossing his lips. It was amazing. Whenever I was down there and Phyllis happened to be inside the house or out shopping for groceries, however, it was a different matter…

"See this goddamn paint job on the house? Isn't this the worst goddamn pile of shit you've ever seen?" I squinted, pressing my nose to the siding to see what he was talking about. It looked fine to me.

"It's only been seven goddamn years, and it already looks like hell. I hired a local guy to paint it. It took him almost a month. He was over here every day, splattering paint around and getting it all over the goddamn windows. Mother had to follow that worthless son of bitch around with a wet rag all day, cleaning up after him. He charged me 500 bucks for this piece of shit. I kept having to call the bastard back over to touch up places he'd missed, and that went on for almost a year. Then he up and moved away. I'd like to get my hands on his fucking neck."

Bill's complaints were mostly about defective products or shoddy workmanship. "Now, we bought this manufactured house direct from the factory back in '08, and the first thing we had go wrong was the goddamn windows. We got double-paned, and the goddamn things got moisture between them right off the bat. That was the worst goddamn year here for rain. It rained every goddamn day. I called them up and told them they better get their asses over here and fix those goddamn windows, or there'd be hell to pay. Well, they got somebody over here and replaced every goddamn one of them with better ones. Didn't charge me a penny. Then Mother had trouble opening some of the new ones they put in, and I'll be goddamn if I didn't have to make them come out and re-replace some of those. It was one goddamn thing after another, let me tell you."

"And last year," Bill droned on, "we had a local outfit come in and rip out all the old carpet in the place and haul it away. Then they installed vinyl flooring. Not a week went by, and I'll be goddamn if it wasn't buckling up in places. I jumped in the truck and drove right to their store. I got up in the manager's face and told that asshole if he didn't fix the floor by the end of the week, I was going to come back there, rip off his head and shit down his neck. I'll tell you what. He had a goddamn crew out the next day. They took out the bad vinyl and installed a whole new goddamn floor while Mother and I played cards at the clubhouse."

"Kind of sounds like you went to hell and back," I quipped.

"Watch the language," Bill chastised, his eyes darting toward the door. "If Mother was here, she'd make you put a quarter in her swears jar." **Hmmm...so that was really how the Cranes put four kids through college.**

Despite his bluster and bravado, I liked Bill. Under the gruff exterior was a good-hearted guy, who had always taken care of his family and friends. Plus, he was a huge dog lover. That was evident when he'd gotten all misty-eyed remembering The Duke.

Most mornings when I walked Sully and Ben, Bill would be sitting in a chair on his patio, waiting for us. As soon as they caught sight of him, the boys' tails would start wagging furiously, and they'd strain at their leashes to get over to him. He bought a box of liver flavor treats, and both of them got one from "Uncle Bill," as I started calling him. Most of the time they were excitable and boisterous around other dogs and humans, but in Uncle Bill's presence they actually behaved. "Sit!" he would command, and all three of us would take a seat.

One morning as we were passing by the Cranes', I noticed two white hairy legs sticking out beyond the arch of the secret garden. I thought for sure Bill had been working back there and had suffered a heart attack or something.

Then I heard a familiar gruff voice mutter "Goddam son of a bitch." It turned out there was a problem with the wiring in the garden and patio area, and Bill couldn't find its source. "Mother's about to have a fit," he told me candidly. "She's planning her Mexican fiesta for next weekend, and I need to get the goddamn wiring fixed or she won't have her fountain and twinkle lights."

"You know, Bill, maybe my old man can help you out with this. He wired all of our houses himself, so he's pretty handy that way."

As soon as the words were out of my mouth, I regretted it. Bill didn't go easy on his contractors or workmen. If my old man couldn't do the repairs, or if he didn't perform them flawlessly, would Bill rip off his head and shit down his neck? I didn't know the answer to that question, but the risk seemed substantial.

"Ok, then that's settled," Bill said, "Tell him to come down here and take a look tomorrow morning. Mother wants to go to those goddamn outlet stores, so he needs to be here before 0900."

When I told him about it, my old man wasn't at all happy that I'd volunteered his services. "Thanks a million," he groused. "Saturday's the only morning I sleep in, and now you've set me up to play advance logistics manager for fucking Custer at the Little Big Horn.

"You better watch your language if moth…I mean, Phyllis, is there," I warned him. "And anyhow, it's more like George C. Scott in **Patton,** when he kicked those goats off the mountain pass for holding up his convoy."

In my mind, I pictured George C. Scott shitting down my old man's neck, and, as usual, I had to hold back the incredible urge to piss myself.

When he got back from Bill and Phyllis's in the morning, my old man went straight to the computer and ordered $20 worth of electrical parts, paying extra for two-day shipping. When I asked him what the problem was with the Cranes' wiring, he shook his head.

"What **isn't** wrong with it? He's got a big jumbled mess of outlets and extension cords, worse than I've ever seen. I mean, it's an electrical fire waiting to happen, and I told him that."

"What did he say?" I asked with trepidation.

"He said a week was plenty enough time for me to get the lights and fountain working before Phyllis's fiesta next weekend. I told him I didn't have everything I needed to do the job, and by God if he didn't tell me get my ass in gear and order them…because *he* didn't want to disappoint *Mother*."

The electrical parts arrived on Monday, and that evening my old man went down to Phyllis and Bill's. They weren't home, but he went ahead and fixed the patio wiring, then switched on the fountain and lighting. They worked. His head and neck hole were out of jeopardy.

Two more days went by, and we didn't hear from Bill or Phyllis, and hadn't seen either of them in their usual haunts. The day before Phyllis's planned fiesta, we were sitting outside when Bill pulled up in his golf cart. Uh oh, I thought, maybe the lights and fountain didn't *stay* fixed.

"Don't get up" Bill ordered from the seat of his EZGO. "I just came down to say thanks for fixing that goddamn wiring. That's a great job you did down there, son. Mother was shickled titless when we got home the other night and her twinkle lights were on and the fountain was working. How much do I owe you Mr. Electrician?"

My old man's chest puffed up like Gomer Pyle getting a commendation from Sergeant Carter. "Nothing at all, Bill," he said, "I was happy to do it for you. "I'll get my payback in sangria and nachos at the fiesta this weekend."

"That's goddamn swell of you, neighbor," Bill said, "But Mother's come down with the flu, and we're going to put a hold on the fiesta until she feels better. Say, that'll give you plenty of time to come down and take a look at a few other electrical problems we've been having. The guy that wired our place was a goddamn moron. If I ever see that idiot again, I'm going to rip off his head and shit down his neck."

Phyllis recovered from her bout with the flu, and the fiesta was a big hit, as all her parties tend to be. In the meantime, my old man solved a few more of Bill's electrical problems and wisely kept his mouth shut about his plumbing know-how.

As the weeks went by, Bill became fonder and fonder of Ben and Sully, particularly Sully. On one occasion, I actually heard him tell Sully he was "Uncle Bill's good boy." I became slightly worried that Uncle Bill might be plotting to kidnap our Sully before he and Phyllis went back to Montana, but as usual, my old man told me I was just being paranoid.

One morning we were late walking by Bill and Phyllis's. Bill had gone over to the clubhouse to play some Texas Hold 'Em with his buddies, and Phyllis was sitting on the patio in Bill's usual spot. The boys made a beeline for her and the bowl of liver treats on the table beside her.

"Listen," Phyllis said, as she distributed the snacks, "We just got a new sofa, and I'm dying for you to see it. I even went out and bought a bunch of new throw pillows for it, and they were darn near as expensive as the couch!"

I really wanted to go in and see the new sofa, but the boys were with me, and Phyllis was a bit of a neat freak. I didn't think it was a real good idea, and I told her so. "Oh, don't be silly," she reassured me. "There's not a darn thing in there the little fellows can hurt. Most everything came from thrift shops or consignment stores."

Inside, the park model was much like Phyllis herself: immaculately groomed and spotlessly clean. The little house was tastefully decorated in coordinated colors and interesting bric a brac. The new sofa was covered in a neutral fabric, and the throw pillows Phyllis had chosen were Navajo weave and must have cost a small fortune. Fresh flowers were in a vase on the dining table.

The boys were behaving like perfect gentlemen, and I relaxed a little and dropped their leashes as I followed Phyllis down the hall to the bedroom. She was showing me a shelf Bill had installed to hold some Mexican pots they'd acquired when I heard a loud thump and scratching noises coming from the front room. Where the hell were the boys? I spun around and tore headlong down the hall.

In the kitchen, a wastebasket was on its side. Coffee grounds, bits of green vegetables and crumpled paper towels littered the vinyl floor. Sully's body was mostly inside the overturned wastebasket. Only his wagging tail protruded, and I could hear vigorous crunching noises coming from within. I ran over and started pulling him out.

He emerged butt first, with the remains of a drumstick clenched firmly between his teeth. I pried it out of his jaws, and was reaching for a paper towel to wipe barbeque sauce off his muzzle, when I heard glorp-glorp sounds coming from the vicinity of the sofa, where Ben was now perched.

Glorping sounds are familiar to anybody who's lived with a dog for many years. They are the noises one hears in the middle of the night, when one's dog is unreachable at the foot of the bed, under the covers, and is on the brink of puking on one's naked feet.

While I'd been singing the praises of Phyllis's decorating skills back in the bedroom, old Ben had been examining the contents of the candy dish on the side table next to the sofa. A few more glorps, and half-chewed M&Ms gushed from his mouth like silver dollars from a one armed bandit. Naturally, the chocolately badness didn't land, as one might have hoped, on the vinyl flooring. Instead, it cascaded like flowing lava onto the tops of Phyllis's new throw pillows, where it began crawling slowly down into the crevasses of the sofa. I stole a glance at Phyllis. She looked like a performer in the third act of a Kabuki tragedy.

I don't fully remember what happened after that, because I hauled the boys back to our trailer and downed several beers, even though it was only about 10:30 in the morning. I told Phyllis I would gladly pay to have the sofa and pillows cleaned, but she graciously declined the offer, telling me not to worry about it. I felt **TERRIBLE**, and the next day I avoided the Cranes' place.

A couple mornings later, Bill was in his regular spot on the patio as I was walking the boys, and he motioned us over. After giving both of them liver treats, he took Sully onto his lap.

"Uncle Bill heard you were a very, very bad boy, Sully," he said.

Sully tilted his head and looked Uncle Bill in the eye. As I watched, Bill's shoulders started to vibrate, and soon his whole body was heaving. Sully, unnerved by the dodgy situation, jumped down from Bill's lap and hid behind my legs. Tears of laughter rolled down Bill's cheeks, and he was unable to speak. Finally, he covered his face with the back of one arm and waved us away.

I think Top Kick might have pissed himself.

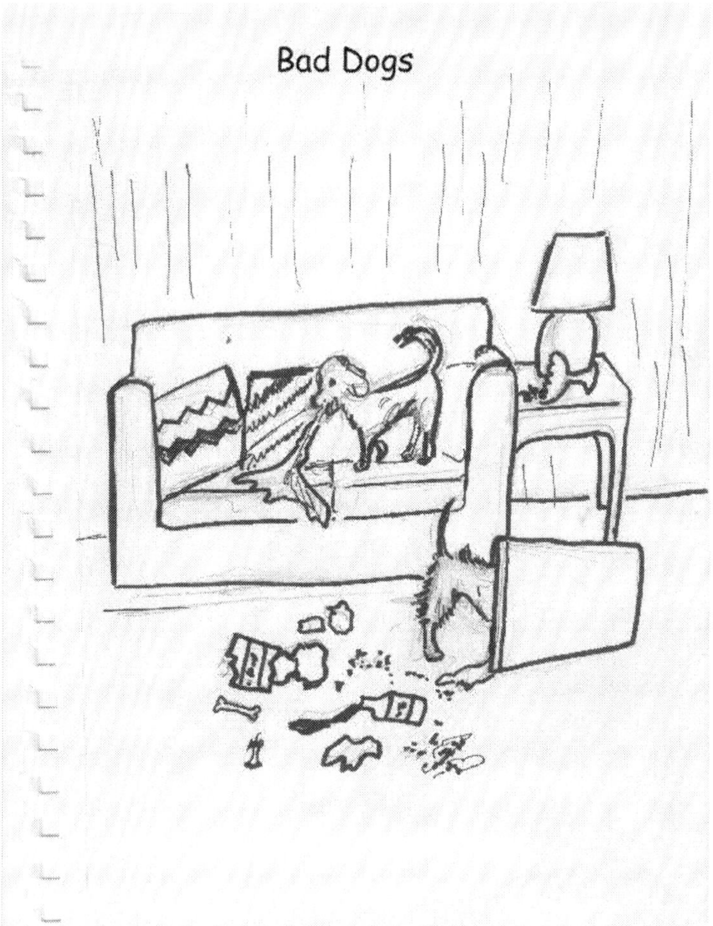
Bad Dogs

Site 24: Me and My Old Man & The Boys

Me and my old man and our two dogs, Sully and Ben, live in a 5th wheel trailer at Site 24. Our fiver is in decent shape for its age. We got a fabulous deal on it, thanks mainly to my negotiating skills with the dopey RV salesman. Ok, so we **have** had to replace a few things on it, like the rooftop AC, the toilet, some of the plumbing, a few lights, hatches, curtains, electrical connections, cabinet doors, mattress, vents, rugs, and my old man had to plug some leaks here and there.

Last week we thought we were going to have to replace the rig's refrigerator, but it turned out to be a light switch thing that had gone haywire, and it only cost $5 to fix. That was like dodging a thousand dollar bullet, so we celebrated by eating at the mall's food court. We both came down with bad cases of The Trotskis, but still and all, we felt blessed by our good fortune with the refrigerator deal.

At the Resort, long-term guests can do anything they want to improve their sites as long as they stay within its allotted boundaries, and as long as Gretchen gives final approval. If a guest builds something on the site, such as a deck or shed, it has to be constructed so that it can be easily dismantled and hauled away when the guest moves out. Some folks have put up fairly elaborate structures on their sites, and many have recirculating fountains, small gazebos, and even portable hot tubs.

We haven't done anything to improve our site except assemble 2 plastic sheds and set out 2 "gravity" chaise lounges that are hard to get out of, but only when you sit on them. I think it has something to do with the force of gravity, but I'm no scientist. We've limited ourselves to minimal improvements because we're still hoping to move away from Lonnie and Daisy May if another site becomes available.

So far, the open sites we've had to choose from, for one reason or another, aren't that much better than the one we're in now, and have even crazier neighbors (than the Mays). Moving a trailer even a couple rows over is a huge pain in the ass, because everything inside has to be secured and locked down. Sewer hoses have to be disconnected and cleaned, then reconnected at the new site; electrical connections have to be re-established; and of course, our two sheds would have to be dismantled and reconstructed, and their contents would have to be moved as well.

It's possible, I suppose, that we'll remain in Site 24 for the rest of our lives. I think I'd rather spend 20 years in a prison cell with Adam Sandler. Ok, maybe not. ***Cruel and unusual punishment***.

Anyhow, you already know a lot about me and my old man and how aggravating he is and how he's a big fucking liar and wants to steal all my profits from ***Trailer Dogs***. You know that we're both dog lovers, and that we treat our dogs like they're our kids because that's what they are, and that if other people don't like it they can kiss our asses. I've also told you about some of the other Trailer Dog dogs who live at the Resort. Now you're just going to have to sit there and read about ***our*** boys, because…altogether now:

It's my book and I'll write what I fucking want to write and there are no refunds.

BEN

Ben's a 9 1/2 pound Yorkie-Poodle mix - a Yorki-Poo. Last March he turned 119 in dog years, which makes him about the same age as some of the geezers at the Resort. He doesn't look his age, though. His teeth are still pretty good, and you can't see any lines or wrinkles on his face because, like most canines' faces, *it has a lot of fur on it*.

Ben's gotten kind of bony in his dotage, but he gets around fine, eats like a Great Dane, and is as demanding as he was when we brought him home at a 6 weeks, and he followed me around for days, squawking at my heels for attention. He had a tiny little body at the time, and a huge round head that made him look like a jack o'lantern. We nicknamed him "Punkin' Haid."

During the first days after we adopted him, Punkin' Haid somehow managed to crawl under the sofa in the family room, despite his monstrous, Ben Affleck - size head. It became his lair, and a refuge from our toy Poodle, Holly, who was a couple years older, and who we figured would whip the new guy into shape and force him to do her will the way she had with us.

Punkin' Haid, as we soon learned, was not about to managed by anyone, including a plump and sassy lady Poodle. He was never aggressive, never snappy or mean with any other creature, man or beast, but when it came to discipline, Punkin' Haid simply ignored anyone who wanted him to do something he did not want to do. He did this with complete good humor, yet in a way that, despite our much larger brains and superior educations, made us think he probably knew best. Punkin' Haid soon won Holly over to his way of thinking, and by then it was too late to try our hand at correcting either one of them.

One afternoon, terrible squawking noises erupted in the family room, and we ran in to see what the commotion was. Punkin' Haid's big head was sticking out from under the sofa, and he was in panic mode, trying to squeeze out the rest of his body, which had become stuck. Holly joined in the caterwauling, and we had to lift the front of the couch to facilitate his escape. He never tried to go under there again, but instead, set up shop under our bed. Soon after, miscellaneous things started to vanish without a trace—the odd shoe, nails and screws from unfinished projects, a pair of gloves carelessly laid aside on a chair, and finally, my old man's favorite flannel shirt.

We looked everywhere for the missing items and were completely baffled, until one afternoon I glimpsed Punkin' Haid, who we'd started calling by his given name, "Ben," disappear under our bed with my new knit scarf trailing behind him. Grabbing a flashlight, I tucked the bed skirt between mattress and box springs, and got down on all fours to have a look. There, amid dust bunnies and little piles of missing contraband, lay Ben, contentedly sucking the fringed edge of the recently pilfered scarf.

Hardly any of the items he'd stashed under the bed were salvageable. My old man's plaid flannel shirt was in the worst shape of all. The pocket was mangled, and all of the buttons were missing. The cuffs had been chewed into masses of dangling threads. The bottom edges of the shirt were still damp from Punkin' Haid's sucking and munching of them, and the damn thing smelled terrible. I washed and dried the miserable rag and gave it back to Ben, hoping it would keep him away from more valuable items. (i.e., my stuff.) We began referring to the monstrosity as "Ben's Toy Shirt."

Whenever we traveled, Ben's Toy Shirt was brought along like a kid's beloved security blanket. It was the first thing we packed, and the first thing we unpacked when we got to our destination. Coming back from a trip to Oregon one year, we accidentally left the shirt behind at a Day's Inn in California.

When we got home, we frantically searched car and luggage to no avail. After a few days without his Toy Shirt, Ben lost interest in looking for it and substituted a section of PVC pipe he found in the yard. He started lugging the pipe around all day, and became so obsessed with it that we started calling him "Tubes." We didn't go back to "Ben" until the day I caught "Tubes" carrying a dried turd in his mouth.

Author's Note: If you must know, despite the fact that he's aggravating and has designs on my book profits, one of the reasons I will stay by my old man's side 'til the bitter end, is this: When we couldn't find Ben's Toy Shirt, I overheard him on the phone with Day's Inn, asking if anyone had turned in a lost flannel shirt from Room 105. Any guy who'd embarrass himself like that for his kid can't be all bad.

Another of Ben's eccentricities is his obsession with human shins. One morning, my old man stepped out of the shower and there was Ben, waiting for him on the bathmat. As my old man dried himself, Ben commenced to painstakingly lick his shins. When he was satisfied that the shins were groomed to perfection, Ben turned and nonchalantly left the bathroom.

Every morning thereafter, Ben appeared at the shower door to attend to his shin lickery enterprise. His services soon expanded to tub bathers, and no matter how quiet I tried to be, and no matter where he was in the house, when he heard the click of the tub's drain opening, Ben would push open the bathroom door and rush over to lick my shins before they could air dry. We finally got used to the process, but houseguests were always surprised/disgusted when Ben barged into the bathroom and began mopping up their extremities. Thankfully, none of our visitors ever admitted to enjoying the process.

Ben's had an amazingly healthy life. Over the years he's only had one or two problems that required the attention of a vet. He had a mild bladder infection when he was about 2, and when he was 9, we noticed a growth on his neck that resembled a pair of testicles. The dangling testicles didn't seem to bother him at all, but when my brother noted that it might be time to buy a jock strap for Ben's new balls, I knew it was time to take action.

The vet offered 3 "estimates," the most expensive of which was $1800 and included a battery of exorbitantly-priced pre-surgical tests and consultations, laser removal of the wart, and a post-operative follow up visit that included toe nail clipping and a bath.

At the time, we were in desperate need of a new pellet stove, so we selected the third and least expensive option, which amounted to taking Ben in one morning to have the growth removed, and bringing him home that same afternoon. It worked out fine, and Ben recovered quickly, warming himself near the new pellet stove while zoned out on pain medication.

Ben doesn't see well now because of cataracts, and his eyes are very sensitive to bright sunlight. I got worried and bought him a pair of dog sunglasses (Doggles) that made him look super cool. Everybody at the Resort made over him and thought he was adorable in the sporty glasses, but the last time I tried to put them on him, he squawked like a goose and tried to bite me. I didn't want to risk causing either of us to stroke out, so I put the Doggles away in a drawer.

Twelve bucks down the drain, but I got really cute pictures of him wearing the Doggles. I read somewhere that some crazy guy spent like 10 grand to have his old dog's cataracts removed. I'm not ***that*** nutty. If I had 10 grand, I'd have my own cataracts removed. If I had 20 grand to spare, though, I'd get my cataracts ***and*** Ben's removed.

When the Doggles didn't work out, I bought Ben a cute little Smokey Bear-type hat for $10. The hat has a wide brim, and a "badge" applique on it." It has a Velcro chin strap and elasticized slots for Ben's floppy ears. When I put it on him, he hated it worse than the goddamn sunglasses. He rolled around on the floor in a tantrum, pawing at the hat until it popped off his giant head like a rock launched from a slingshot. Then he sat there glaring at me, and daring me to try to put it on him again. I finally gave up and tossed him a treat to stop the pouting.

Another $10 down the drain. Ben seems to think we should pop for the cataract surgery and lose the sunglasses/hat approach. Actually, it might be cheaper in the long run.

A while back, Ben seemed a little out of sorts, so I made an appointment at the vet's to see if it was anything serious. I brush the boys' teeth religiously, and the night before, Ben had squawked and fought me off when I put the toothbrush in his mouth. He was usually very cooperative with tooth-brushing, which I'd been doing for about 16 years.

The vet stuck a thermometer in his butt (Ben's butt, not the vet's butt), listened to his heart and lungs, palpated his abdomen, and felt all around inside his mouth. While the vet was examining his mouth, Ben sat there, perfectly behaved, with a little halo floating above his enormous Affleckian head.

"Everything looks fine," the vet told me. "Ben's heart is strong, his lungs are clear, and he doesn't have a temperature. Frankly, I've never seen a dog this old in as good condition. What's the problem?" I described the squawking and kicking when I'd tried to brush Ben's teeth, and how he'd never done anything like that before. "Did you do anything different than usual?" the vet asked.

"Not really," I replied. "We ran out of the poultry-flavored dog toothpaste I usually use, so I substituted the same brand, only in mint flavor."

The vet turned to me with the same incredulous expression Ben had for the sunglasses and Smokey Bear hat. "Well, **there's** your problem," he said, shaking his head in disbelief at my simplemindedness.

"Obviously he doesn't like mint-flavored toothpaste. Ben was trying to show you how disgusted he was that you didn't know any better than to switch flavors on him like that. You need to buy him some more of the kind of toothpaste he prefers. We have it in stock at the desk. Rose will add it to your bill."

Before I left the office, Ben's unnecessary vet visit had cost around $75, for the exam and dog toothpaste. Sadly, they were out of the poultry-flavored kind, so Rose substituted a vanilla-flavored paste, which, she assured me, "all the dogs just love."

Not our Ben. The little bastard held out until we broke down and had his special poultry-flavored toothpaste overnighted from Amazon. $75 for the vet, plus the cost of having the poultry-flavored toothpaste shipped. I'm happy to report that Ben seems satisfied - for the time being. On the bright side, his breath smells like a bucket of KFC.

A lot of people would say/have said/do say that we've spoiled Ben horribly, but me and my old man don't see it that way. We don't believe we're entirely responsible for his behavior any more than parents of human children think they're responsible when their kid posts their sex tape on the internet.

Frankly, all of our dogs have been largely untrainable and badly behaved, conduct we always blamed on the people we got them from when they were puppies. Since we started adopting neglected or abused rescues, that explanation doesn't hold up quite as well. Of course, we don't really give a shit what people think of us or our dogs, unless they force the issue by giving **Trailer Dogs** a bad review, which will cause everyone in the whole world to hate them as well.

Grumpy Ben

SULLY

We adopted Sully in 2013, a month after Cheekly the Chihuahua died, and two weeks after saying a final goodbye to our precious 15-year old Poodle, Holly. Holly had been suffering from congestive heart failure for over a year, and we'd tried to move heaven and earth to save her. No remedy worked for long, and the vet advised us that it was "time."

All three of us, Ben included, were overwhelmed with grief. Me and my old man felt like nothing would ever be the same, that we might never be happy again. Ben, who as I said earlier, had always been in robust health, suddenly seemed old and frail. Even his usual keen interest in toys had dried up. I'd catch the old boy sitting by the French doors in the living room, not even bothering to bark when a bird happened to land on the porch right in front of him.

Having experienced this kind of acute heartache in the past, we discussed getting another dog - a rescue like Cheekly - to keep Ben company, and to have something positive to focus our attentions on. We agreed it was too soon.

We had a multitude of problems we were struggling with, like a crumbling business that was occupying our minds day and night, and which was causing severe financial stress on our rapidly dwindling savings. How could we possibly take on the added responsibility of caring for and rehabilitating another dog, given our current crises and burdens that were already threatening to crush us?

Two weeks later, as I was perusing the same dog rescue internet site where we'd found Cheekly, I spotted Sully, who was described as a "Schnauchi" - a Schnauzer-Chihuahua mix. Looking back, Sully was an unlikely candidate for us at the time. For one thing, I was pining for Holly so terribly, that all I could think about was finding another girl dog exactly like the one we'd just lost. In truth, I was so distraught, that had I possessed the finances, and had cloning been an option, well…

In the summary of his rescue, Sully was described as a high-strung male stray who had been wandering city streets for several days, possibly abandoned by an owner who could no longer afford –or wanted- to care for him. After someone called to report they'd seen a larger dog attack Sully, animal control came and managed to capture him after a long, intense chase. Sully was then taken to a shelter. He had no collar and there was no ID chip in his ear. His back had been ripped open by the other dog, and he needed stiches to close the wound.

Within days, Sully was neutered, vaccinated for Parvo, Distemper and Rabies, and given an injection to prevent Kennel Cough. The Kennel Cough vaccine made him very ill, and he was put on antibiotics. When no one came forward to claim him, a woman with a local rescue group reimbursed the shelter for his care, and took him home with her. The rescue summary said that, based on an examination of his teeth by a veterinarian, Sully was approximately two or three years old, and in good health.

In the picture of Sully, taken from the side, his ribs were protruding and he was extremely thin. His salt & pepper coat was short and dull, and along his spine, toward his rat-like tail, a row of spiky fur stood up like a shark's fin over the scar from the dog attack. I couldn't tell from the picture exactly how big Sully was, but he had 4 long stick legs that made him look like he was on stilts.

A picture of Sully taken from the front was even more disturbing. His ears were huge, and stuck straight up from his head, which had a few scraggly long hairs sprouting from it. His mouth was slightly ajar, revealing a slight underbite that gave him a goofy, "what, me-worry?" grin.

I might have passed him up then and there had it not been for his tail, which was blurred in the photo. Despite all Sully had been through, *his tail had been wagging when the picture was taken*. This was definitely a dog worth rescuing. And who knew…maybe Sully would end up rescuing us as well.

I called the rescue organization and was told that Sully would be among the potential adoptees at the pet store the following Saturday. Me and my old man were first in line when the store opened.

Sully was lying down in a cage when we first saw him. He seemed listless and depressed, and not interested in anything going on around him. I picked him up, and his skinny body was so rigid that it was almost like he'd turned to stone. He turned his head away from me and looked over my shoulder as I stroked the wiry fur on his back. I told him what a handsome boy he was, that we were his new mom and dad, and that we were going to take him home to meet his brother, Ben. The formerly silent tail began to wag once again.

When we got Sully home, he and Ben made a cursory inspection of each other, and when they were finished, Ben loped off into the other room. For the first time in weeks, he went to his toy basket and rummaged around, finally selecting Mr. Weasel, his favorite. Sully watched intently as Ben, head held high, trotted past him and deposited

Mr. Weasel in his bed, where he commenced to chew and suck on the toy, keeping one watchful eye on the stranger.

In the first weeks, all of us had a difficult period of adjustment. Sully hadn't quite recovered from his ordeal and experience at the shelter, when he developed a mild infection in the stitches from his neutering. More antibiotics cleared that up fairly quickly. I had to be careful about feeding him too much, despite my desire to put some meat on his bones. His system simply wouldn't tolerate a lot of food at one sitting, no matter how ravenous he was.

Sully also had the disconcerting habit of "marking" his food dish after he'd eaten, so as to keep Ben away from it. When he started pissing on Ben's dish as well, I began feeding them separately, and tossing both dishes in the sink as soon as they'd finished eating. I was less certain what to do about their male competiveness, when one day I saw Ben lift his leg on the bottom of the sofa, and Sully followed suit by peeing in the same spot. I bought a package of boy dog diapers (belly bands), and got out the steam cleaner. It was going to be a long haul.

At first, Sully's standoffishness and mistrust of our intentions was a little hard to take. He would not, no matter how much we coaxed him with sweet talk and savory treats, take food from our hands. We'd toss a treat in his direction and he'd snap it up and then dash off to the other room to eat it. If we bent down to pet him, he'd run from us and try to hide. He refused to sit on either of our laps for more than a second or two, and he'd get up four or five times in the middle of the night to roam the house. I finally had to start closing the bedroom door when we turned in.

Sully was a restless and fearful little dog, and not quite ready to fully commit to a strange new family and way of life. He was especially anxious around human males, and would run from my old man the minute he walked through the door.

Although he would sometimes growl softly at men he didn't know, Sully was usually so quiet that we thought maybe he couldn't bark. Then one day the UPS guy came to the door. It just goes to show how wrong a person can be. Sully's actual bark, a piercing whoop/howl, is enough to make your milk curdle.

We found out the hard way that Sully was also a bit of an escape artist, in that when something scared him, he could execute a backflip and pull out of his collar in a millisecond. We tried putting him in a harness, but he chewed up the first three, so we went back to a collar, keeping it as snug as we dared without cutting off his air.

Over time, Ben and Sully developed a friendship, and the two became inseparable. It took more time for Sully to trust the human members of the pack, but after about three months, I started having to force him *off* my lap in order to restore circulation in my legs and ease the cramps in my hands from massaging him for 30 minutes at a time. He loved to be groomed and fussed over. He put on weight and became playful, getting into the toy basket (when Ben wasn't looking) to chew on Mr. Foxtail and Mr. Weasel.

Sully's coat filled out and grew sleek and shiny from all the vitamins and grooming. He came to us when we called him, and took food directly from our outstretched hands. When my old man had to go to California on business, we were satisfied that at last the tide had turned. The boys were fine on the road trip, and Sully seemed to enjoy looking out the window at passing scenery, occasionally barking/growling at the occupants of cars that whizzed by us on the freeway.

We checked into a motel in Livermore, CA, and got a room on the second floor next to the elevator. Sully refused to go anywhere near it, so when I took the boys out to do their business, I had to pick him up and carry him down the stairs. (He was also afraid of stairs.) At the bottom of the stairwell was an exit door leading directly to the parking lot, and during our stay, I used the same route to walk the boys at least four times a day.

We were returning from a walk one afternoon when I saw a woman at the hatchback of her SUV across the parking lot. A dog's crate was visible, and I watched as she attached the end of a leash to the dog inside the crate. Without warning, the dog, a large hound of some kind, burst out of the crate and headed straight for us. In the same instant, Sully did a back flip, slipped out of his collar, and took off across the parking lot in the opposite direction of the charging dog.

I watched in horror as the hound raced toward us, and I knew instinctively that he was going after Sully. Somehow, I managed to plant my foot on the dog's trailing leash as he darted by, and the hound came to an abrupt stop. His owner, out of breath and apologetic, rushed over and took charge of him.

There was no sign of Sully anywhere. A busy freeway was on the other side of a chain link fence. Almost paralyzed with shock and fear, I picked Ben up and rushed toward the motel's side entrance. As I rounded the corner of the building, the first thing I saw was Sully. He was sitting on the concrete landing, leaning against the glass entry door. He was waiting for us.

I put Ben down, picked Sully up, and with a shaky hand, slid my card key into the slot. The green light flashed, and we were inside, safe at last. I carried Sully into the elevator as Ben plodded along beside us. Back in our room, I fell on the bed and gathered the boys in close to me. We were all trembling. This happened over three years ago, and I vaguely recall that one of us wept a little.

About three or four weeks after we got back from the trip, I was walking Sully and Ben around our ranch property when a cottontail rabbit jumped from behind a bush and ran down the path ahead of us. Sully took off after it, pulling his leash from my hands. I yelled "stop," and to my utter astonishment, he halted dead in his tracks, sat down, and waited for us to catch up.

Sully has never run from either one of us since. He knows that we are his pack, and that we will protect him, and each other, from any outside threat. He is one of the sweetest, most affectionate dogs we've ever had, and I can say in all candor that he helped to rescue me and my old man and Ben from one of the worst periods of our lives.

We're Trailer Dogs living at Site 24. By all means, come and visit us. But when you do, make sure you come in peace.

A Trailer Dog's Alarm Clocks

CHAPTER 5

TRAILER GODS

I estimate that about 95% of Trailer Dogs at the Resort consider themselves to be "good Christians." This belies the fact that they don't attend church, and think tithing is what a baby does when it's growing teeth. But "religious" Trailer Dogs know their Bible, and always manage to pull up an appropriate quote, especially when it furnishes an easy out or convoluted explanation for some shit they've just pulled.

My old man was born and raised Catholic. Like most former Papists, he'll be the first to tell you that these days, while he no longer fears God per se, he still has recurring nightmares about being attacked by hordes of black widow spiders, wearing wire-rimmed glasses and armed with plastic rulers.

I, on the other hand, was raised mostly southern Baptist by a widowed mother who believed that threatening me with Eternal Damnation was the *only* sure way to get me to put away my Davy Crockett Alamo fort, turn off the TV and get my ass to bed. Mom was wrong of course, but that didn't stop her from trying.

We lived in a tiny house in a neighborhood of equally tiny, post-WWII houses. None of them were that much bigger than some of the travel trailers and RVs we see tearing down the highways today. All of the houses had TV antennas sprouting from their roofs, and kids, who on Saturday mornings could be found sitting on cold linoleum floors, lapping up Kellogg's Sugar Corn Pops and watching Cartoon Carnival on the old Stewart Warner or Philco TV. My peers and I all ate the same thing every day, because, as the commercials drummed into our skulls, **The pops are sweeter and the taste is new, they're shot with sugar, through and through.** Sugar Pops were tops, the TV told us. And we believed it.

My favorite cartoon was Casper the Friendly Ghost. Don't ask me *why* Casper was my favorite. I've always had a mild obsession with death, but that's not really important to this story, so forget I even said anything.

Around 9 or so on Saturdays, Mom would come in and stand between me and the Philco to say it was time to get ready for Vacation Bible School. I despised VBS for a number of reasons, not the least of which was that it interrupted the Cartoon Carnival marathon (which lasted until noon) and forced me behave for an hour or two. At church. On a *Saturday*. What the hell was I, a Seventh Day Adventist?

One morning, after a particularly inspiring episode of Casper, as I was carrying my empty cereal bowl to the kitchen, I made up a little song on the spot. Innocently, I sang it to the tune of Casper's bouncy theme song:

Casper, the holy ghost, the holiest ghost you know...

From out of nowhere Mom swooped down on me like Dracula cutting line at a blood bank. "Do you know what you've done?" she asked me nervously, her eyes wide with incomprehension and something akin to righteous fear.

"I was just singing the Casper song", I said, unnerved by her seriousness, and trying to quickly deduce what the problem was so I could bullshit my way out of trouble. I figured it probably had something to do with blasphemy, though. In our house, the winds of eternal damnation were always blowing in my direction. "It's just what they sing on TV, Mom. It's ok."

"No, it is **not** ok," Mom said in the same frantic voice Carrie's lunatic mother used when she ranted about her daughter's "dirty pillows" and caused Carrie to burn the house down and kill all her shithead high school classmates.

"What you were doing was blasphemy - comparing the Holy Ghost to a cartoon character. That's an unpardonable sin in the eyes of God." She went even further. "You could **kill** someone, and God would still forgive you if you repented. You could lie and cheat and steal and covet your neighbor's wife, and God would still forgive you. But forgive you for mocking the Holy Ghost? I'm afraid **that** He cannot and will not do."

I sucked in my breath. I'd never been in a pickle like this before with The Almighty. I was 8 years old, and hadn't, as yet, killed anybody. Sure, there'd been lots of times when I'd tampered with the fate of my immortal soul by stealing change from Mom's purse and lying about it, but none of the sins I'd committed so far were **this** irreversible.

As for coveting our neighbor's wife, Mrs. Lindenschmidt was 82, and chased me and my friends with a broom if we so much as cut across her driveway. (That old gal could run.) Plus, she had warts and hair on her upper lip. I wasn't sure exactly what "covet" was, but if it meant wishing Mr. Lindenschmidt's wife would drop dead, I was probably in even bigger trouble than I'd thought.

That night I got down on my knees and prayed like I'd never prayed before:

Dearest God, I had no idea what I was doing, mocking the Holy Ghost like that. I'm sorry. I'm just a kid, Lord. And plus, I thought Casper was a ghost-angel or something like that. He's always doing nice deeds for people, and sometimes a halo appears over his head. Or maybe it's a light bulb when he has a good idea, God. I'm not real sure about the halo. But whatever that thing is, I don't think I should have to burn in Hell for all eternity just because I didn't know about the Holy Ghost rule, which I just found out about this morning. Please accept my deepest apology and forgive me. Amen.

It seemed to me the prayer was pretty solid, but I was still really worried. I couldn't get to sleep for thinking about burning in Hell. Maybe my prayer, earnest though it was, wasn't going to get me out of this scrape. I'd heard somewhere that ignorance of the law was not an acceptable defense. And that was just in human civil matters, not in God's heavenly courtroom. I tossed and turned and agonized until, deprived of all rest, I entered a state of delirium. The blasphemous Casper song kept popping back into my head, uninvited, like an unholy earworm:

Casper, the holy ghost, the holiest ghost you know...

It was like I was possessed. First I'd think about the song, then I'd start asking God's forgiveness again for my wickedness. I was doomed and I knew it. I'd committed the unpardonable sin again and again, as though I was determined to strike the match myself and burn in Hell for eternity. This went on all night long.

Sunday morning, Mom took the thermometer out of my mouth and said I was running a high fever and was too sick to go to church. Oh great, I thought, I'll die here alone and unforgiven, and go straight to Hell. And I'm already on fire. My eyeballs and throat were burning like Shamrock, Meshack and Albinigo in Nebengeezer's fiery furnace.

I spent the remainder of that Sunday drifting in and out of consciousness. I asked God to send me a sign I'd been forgiven for my unforgivable sin, but nothing happened except I ate some ice chips and threw up a couple times. My fever broke that night, about the same time measles popped out all over my body. Within a few days I started to feel a lot better, and I was sure God had cured me as sign of His forgiveness. I was euphoric and light-headed just to be alive. I began to hum a little tune

Casper the something ghost...the somethingest ghost you know...

Mom and I were incredibly close, but we never spoke of the Holy Ghost event again. I'm not sure if she realized the anguish it caused me, but if she did, she was of the old school in child-rearing and probably thought it did me good. A few years later we stopped going to the Baptist church and started attending a Methodist church in an adjoining neighborhood.

The Methodists were much more to my liking. There was no Vacation Bible School, and Methodists were less excitable than the Baptists. I didn't have to attend Sunday School and could catch up on my weekend sleep in the quiet, peaceful comfort of air conditioned pews during the church service without having to worry about being forced into the baptismal tank. The moral of this story is: God is love and forgiveness. Just don't fuck with the Holy Ghost if you know what's good for you.

The Bible is not a favorite book of mine like it is with Donald Trump and George W. Bush, who cling to it like a tick would a hemorrhoid. I'm not implying that God didn't know how to write a book, because that would be blasphemy, and I'm still a little worried about spending time in Hell on that rap. But I would be bearing false witness if I failed to point out that when Martha Stewart came along with "Good Things," her cooking/writing skills knocked The Good Book right out of first place as the number one coffee table book in the world. Maybe it's just me, but this never would have happened if the Bible had included a few decent recipes that didn't involve fish.

I do not think I'm being overly critical or risking my immortal soul when I point out that God apparently didn't have the self-discipline or time to put His own thoughts to paper. As history tells us, human guys, like Matthew, Luke and Samson, did the heavy lifting when it came to writing down the Almighty's thoughts and rules.

My point is: despite all the begetting, reading the Bible can be a real slog if you don't knock back a few cold ones before you dig in. It could have been much improved by righteous editing and a firm elbow on the delete key.

Which brings up the question of why God didn't invent computers and word processing <u>before</u> the Bible was written? That opens the door as to why He didn't invent electricity back then as well. Makes you wonder, doesn't it?

One more point about God, and then maybe I'll move on to a more interesting topic. I often wonder why God didn't just create the Bible on some gold tablets - like he did the 10 Commandments - and hide them in the Garden of Eden, or maybe even somewhere in upstate New York?

Adam and Eve, Native Americans in this scenario, would have eventually stumbled across them like bewildered contestants on ***Survivor*** looking for the tiki idol. If they'd had a Bible to guide them, maybe they would have had a better idea about what was in store for them, with white people coming in and stealing all their corn from the Garden, and then slaughtering them by the thousands.

Maybe they could have made themselves attractive clothes and something more comfortable to sleep in than fig leaf loincloths. I suppose that would have led to more begetting, and that would have eventually caused over-population and Global Warming, and *remind self to complete this train of thought when not drunk*.

In conclusion, there's a whole lot of sex in the Bible, mainly because the guys in there were doing a whole lot of fooling around. That's why they had to call sex "begetting," because "begetting" was okay, whereas fucking multiple wives, girlfriends, neighbors' wives, slaves and the occasional camel, was more or less frowned upon back then. Today, however, it's considered acceptable behavior in male-dominated societies worldwide.

Church Lady

The woman me and my old man call "Church Lady" is another of the Resort's holier-than-us denizens, and I say that with humility that comes from knowing that everyone we meet is more religious than we are. She lives full time in a 5th wheel trailer, two rows over from us. The ***one and only*** time I have seen who I assumed was Church Lady's husband, he was going back inside their trailer. He was old, and seemed a tad on the feeble side.

The first time I encountered Church Lady herself, she was sitting in a lawn chair next to her trailer, reading the Bible. I knew it was the Bible because it was big and black, and had those onion skin pages me and my cousin ripped out and rolled our doobies in back in the day.

The Bible was studded with dozens of fluttering yellow Post-it tabs, and Church Lady was making copious notes on a stenographer's pad balanced on the arm of her chair. As me and the dogs passed by, she looked up briefly and nodded in our direction, then returned to her note taking.

I didn't get a good look at Church Lady's face, but her white hair was swept up in a neat bun at the back of her head. She was wearing a shapeless cotton dress and had on shoes that looked like the stocky, lace-up "Enna Jetticks" my grandma used to wear. She seemed prim and very proper.

Every day thereafter, Church Lady and I exchanged nods and waves when I walked by her trailer. She was always reading the Bible and making notes. The yellow Post-it slips were multiplying faster than the Dugger Family, high on fertility drugs and porn. By the time the boys and I finished our walk and circled back around the Resort, Church Lady had disappeared, her lawn chair neatly folded and leaning against the trailer. One morning during our walk, Ben slowed to a stop, arranged his legs in the ubiquitous dog poop stoop, and commenced to do his business close to the front of Church Lady's trailer.

Here, skeptical Reader, I must inform you of something so bizarre, I insist you google it just to prove to yourself I'm not lying through my teeth on this occasion. In the future I'll alert you to google things whenever I feel it's warranted - otherwise, there's no need for you to waste your wifi minutes fact-checking any statements you may have misgivings about.

The model of Church Lady's trailer is INFERNO. If you followed my above instructions about googling, you now know this is the gospel truth. You can't make up shit that improbable unless you were one of the guys who wrote about begetting in the Bible, with the hope of convincing everyone that God **ordered** you to boink 12-year old slave girls, and that your old lady was ok with it.

Anyhow, as Ben was straining to release the last of his intestinal package, I heard a woman's voice inside the belly of the Inferno. Swear words were involved, as was the taking of the Lord's name in vain. "Goddam son-of-a-bitch, where the hell is it?" the voice raged, "I thought we put it in the Bible." A few seconds passed when a man's voice - or what sounded like a man - said "I don't feel so good…I forgot where I put it."

"You'd forget your dick if it wasn't semi-attached," the woman's hostile voice continued. "Now, where is that goddamn cash? Rent's due in a few days and we don't want Gretchen snooping around here, stirring up shit, do we?" That was all I heard of the argument, and the next day when Church Lady, nose buried in Bible, nodded at me and executed a friendly little wave, I thought I might have dreamed the whole thing.

And maybe I did. Six months have gone by, and Church Lady is still here. She still reads the Bible in the mornings and waves at us. Sometimes I see her smoking during her Bible study, and one time I'd swear I saw her pull out a flask and take a swig from it. I haven't seen hide nor hair of her sickly husband, though, and that troubles me. But not enough to go snooping around there, stirring up shit. Because sometimes when shit happens, you have to figure it's just God's will.

CHAPTER 6

THE TRAILER DOG DIET

Favorite Recipes

I know it's strange for me to start out with this personal anecdote in the Trailer Dog Diet chapter, but again, blah blah blah … my book … blah blah … my decision … blah … end of story. **I HATE TUNA**. My hatred for what I think of as canned barf on a cracker may have something to do with the dietary child abuse that used to go on in the Catholic Church. As you have already seen, I do not shy away from social topics no matter how explosive they might be, or how little I may actually know about them.

As you also already know, I wasn't raised Catholic, so I escaped this widespread mistreatment. But my old man was, and a lot of my friends were too. Every Friday, Catholic kids were denied Whoppers and Big Macs, and were forced by their brain-washed, abusive parents to eat some reeking casserole concoction that had tuna in it. I don't know how they swallowed that stuff without a milkshake chaser, but I suppose the prospect of burning in Eternal Hell was just as terrifying to them as frying in Hades for singing the Casper song was for me. I felt sorry for the Catholic kids, but my sympathy was diminished by all the "holy days" they got off from school. In my mind, those holy days more than made up for the tuna abuse.

Priests and nuns and bishops and popes were complicit. They stood by and let it happen. I don't enjoy condemning a whole belief system. I just lay out the facts, and let people make up their own minds. But any religion that compels children to eat nasty food should be put out of business, and that includes Quakers, who for millions of years have forced their progeny to eat oatmeal without benefit of brown sugar.

As much as I know it is a tool of Satan, I make tuna salad for dinner occasionally, but only if it's too hot to mic a frozen burrito, or on nights when I'm worn out from surfing the net all day. All that's really needed for my recipe is a large can of tuna and a can opener. I toss the tuna into a bowl, mix in a little mayo and a half-cup of dried onion flakes to help cut the smell.

For a vegetable, I serve the tuna salad alongside a box of crackers flavored with rosemary. Even so, my old man, who still bears psychological scars from his exploitation by uncompromising, emaciated nuns, cannot choke down a plate of my homemade tuna salad without getting hammered first. Thanks, Obama.

In cold weather, I may substitute toast for the crackers, and if I'm feeling culinarily adventurous, I'll heat up a can of tomato soup to go with it. Tomato soup is a good accompaniment to tuna dishes, because after the diners are finished eating, they can soak their reeking tuna fingers in the leftover soup. This is a tip you'll ***never*** find in a Martha Stewart cookbook, but it's as effective as dousing your dog with tomato juice after a skunk encounter.

The Scientific Project

For the sake of reporting fully on the Trailer Dogs' diet, I decided to research the subject by examining the contents of the Resort's dumpsters the same way Sigourney Weaver did when she poked her nose around in gorilla crap during her portrayal of the world famous zoologist, Dian Fossey, in the movie ***Gorillas in the Mist***.

I allowed my old man to assist me in the project in return for my allowing him to assist me in the project. Our - well, ***his***, first order of business was to open up the dumpster nearest to our trailer so I could view the detritus therein. This task was somewhat difficult for me, as the dumpster's unpleasant tang made impossible for me get within ten feet of it. Plan B called for my old man to remove bags of garbage from the dumpster, then untie and open them up. I would then look at the contents, and enter the details in my notebook.

Sadly, the Plan B approach also proved too overwhelming for my sensitive olfactory apparatus, so I resorted to Plan C, wherein I tossed the notebook and pen to my old man and ran back to our trailer, leaving him to sort through the reeking piles and to compile a list of the garbage he found. Regrettably, he was unable to repeat the process in the area of the Resort where Canadians gather, as the stench from their dumpster was too overpowering even for a man with his tolerance for bad odors.

The following are my findings from the project. It is important to note that the Resort dumpsters had been emptied by Waste Management the previous day, so the items inside had been deposited within approximately 24 hours of my scientific investigation. However, to ensure that my efforts are not ridiculed by the scientific community, I should add that Trailer Dogs don't always dispose of their refuse according to any pre-determined schedule. Many times it will sit in a bag outside their trailer for days at a time, until it is detected by crows and turkey buzzards, or Lonnie May.

DUMPSTER 1 CONTENTS

17 empty potato chip bags in varying flavors, including "Biscuits and Gravy"

20 empty corn chip bags, in varying flavors

6 empty pretzel bags – sticks, rods, minis, sourdough nuggets

36 empty bags of Cheetos, 26 fried and 10 baked

48 empty bags of Doritos - super hot, cool, lukewarm

8 empty boxes of Crunch & Munch

32 wrappers from frozen burritos

2 empty jars of peanut butter, crunchy and smooth

15 empty Spam cans

1 package of wieners, 2 wieners remaining

72 beer cans

3 empty wine boxes

1 empty whiskey bottle

2 empty tequila bottles, dried up worms intact

30 Ho Ho wrappers

14 Hostess fried pie wrappers

3 mud pie ice cream sandwich boxes, empty

3 M&Ms bags, 2 peanut, 1 plain, empty

4 ripped open pizza boxes

6 full-size garbage bags filled with raw vegetables, in varying stages of decay

23 Chef Boyardee Beef Ravioli cans, empty

1 empty tuna can (probably responsible for the dumpster's overpowering stench)

DUMPSTER 2 (Canadians)

n/a

SCIENTIFIC CONCLUSION

Many of the items in DUMPSTER 1, with the exception of the empty tuna can, appear to have come from our own trailer. Based on my investigation, I concluded that me and my old man need to cut down on our purchase of fresh vegetables, as they only go to waste and have to be thrown out. I also concluded that someone in our section of the Resort is eating a lot of Spam, which is extremely high in sodium, and which should be avoided for health reasons.

CHAPTER 7

AMY SCHUMER'S PANTIES

In the previous chapter, I discussed Trailer Dogs' diet and food preferences and presented irrefutable scientific research. Now, you may be scratching your heads and/or undercarriages, wondering what in the hell Amy Schumer's panties have to do with the next part of the book, and why would I devote a whole chapter to the subject of a comedian's undergarments.

I wish I had time to explain it to you, but **Room** came from Netflix today, and I need to get this section done so I can watch it in peace and not have to be at your beck and call 24-7. For people who paid so little for this kind of quality reading entertainment, you sure can be a pain in the ass. Read on and see for yourself what the connection is, assuming there is one, which there may not be for all I know. Life is like that. You have to take risks sometimes. Gah.

Relying on facts and figures that will back me up, over seven-eighths of Trailer Dogs (at least in the Resort) qualify as seriously overweight. To put it in nicer terms that won't offend any of my lardy readers, one-eighth of the Trailer Dogs living in the Resort -- if they lost 30-40 pounds -- would be of *almost* normal size. I include myself in this group, so don't go getting your big noses out of joint like Amy Schumer did when she was callously referred to as "plus-size" by some people who had seen her in person.

Authors Note: I could have said "getting your panties in a bunch" in that last sentence instead of "getting your big noses out of joint." It would have been funnier, but I felt it was sexist.

What caused Amy's meltdown happened after she'd posed with other plumpishly fat female entertainers in **Glamour Magazine**. I don't have all the sordid details, but apparently the editorial staff labeled the entire group "plus-size," and Amy took great offense at being included. She fired back at her tormenters with a withering response in which she informed them that she **WAS NOT**, by any stretch of the imagination, **PLUS-SIZE**. She went on to say that she weighed around 160 pounds, wore a Size 6, and she implied that she got plenty of action in the old humpty-dumpty, smoochy-coochy, fucky-ducky department, if you catch my drifty.

As I've privately *and* publicly stated, Amy Schumer is an entertainer I adore, despite the fact that her uncle, NY Senator Chuck Schumer, is an elitist prick. I have no doubt that if George Clooney wasn't already married to that skinny-ass lady lawyer, he'd jump Amy's bones in a heartbeat. But when I read what Amy wrote about wearing Size 6 and *not* being plus-size, I had to laugh. And not in a good, Amy-Schumer-just-made-me-piss-myself sort of way.

It's obvious to me that Amy is woefully ignorant of the NEW RULES for the millennia:

- Orange is the new black
- 70 is the new 50

- Billionaire Democrats are the new billionaire Republicans (and vice versa)
- Size 6 is the new Size 16

Amy isn't to blame for not understanding that she's been forced onto the plus-size side of the scales, despite the fact that she may currently be drowning in a Size 6 from Saks Fifth Avenue. If she had to buy her clothes at Walmart like women in Trailer Dog World, she'd for damn sure need a 16 in just about everything *except* underwear.

In Trailer Dog World, Amy's panties would be XXL, whereas in Amy Schumer's Saks Fifth Avenue World, she probably gets by with XXSM. In Trailer Dog World, Amy's panties would come rolled up tight, like little pink, yellow, and blue sausages, 10 to a Ziploc bag. And the bag wouldn't be lined with tissue paper and have "Victoria's Secret" printed on it either.

All of our clothing is made in other countries these days (just ask Trump where he gets his clothing line manufactured), and I guess it's impossible for foreign garment workers to comprehend that a pair of denim jeans that comfortably fits the average American woman could house a family of five in their Bangkok neighborhoods.

This unfairness pisses the Bankokians off so much, that they *deliberately* make *all* women's pants five sizes smaller than called for by the patterns. Then the teeny tiny pants are shipped to US markets under the "Lady Shamu" brand. Lady Shamu's Size 4 pants, for example, would be a perfect fit for a morbidly obese female in Bangladesh. But here in America, even Calista Flockhart couldn't squeeze her microscopic ass into them.

I seriously doubt Amy Schumer will ever be brought so low that her dainties come from a clearance bin at Walmart, but with guys like her Uncle Chuck running the show, who's to say it can't happen? I'm sorry if she suffered damage to her self-esteem by a discussion of her underwear in **Trailer Dogs**, but Amy, you should know by now, this is America, and there's freedom of speech, and it's my book, and I'll write about whatever the fuck I want to.

As to the question of why so many Trailer Dogs, along with their Trailer Dog dogs, are overweight, I have a theory that it has something to do with how much we eat and how little we exercise. Some days, the only exercise I get is when I walk the boys to the clubhouse to see if there's Halloween candy left in the bowl.

Or maybe it's a sluggish thyroid gland that on weekends causes my hands to wrap themselves around a foot-long cheesesteak sub with all the trimmings, and French fries for dessert. My thyroid has gotten so out of whack lately that it's been forcing me to eat the same stuff during the week that I graze on over the weekend. And during the holidays, it's like the damn thing goes into hibernation and doesn't wake up until after Easter, when it's had its fill of those fucking Cadbury eggs.

When Christmas had come and gone, me and my old man realized we'd gained a few pounds. Well, ok, more than a *few* pounds. Truth is, our fiver was listing to port about 20 degrees when we both sat on the same side. Our concerns multiplied when the tripod holding up the front end of the rig appeared to have sunk about 3 inches into the ground. What to do, what to do? We ruled out a couple things right off the bat:

DIETS

Diets don't work. We all know that. We're not sure *why* they don't work, but experts say they don't, and that's good enough for us. Some diets sound ok on paper, but when you start peeling all those fruits and vegetables and dunking your bagels in yogurt instead of cream cheese…well…'nuff said. Here's the deal. Diets don't allow you to eat the shit you want to eat in the quantities you want to eat it. I don't know why it took a bunch of over-educated dweebs 2 years and 5 million in grants to figure that one out.

JUICING

Colon cleansing only works for people like Gwyneth Paltrow, whose intestinal contents don't amount to a hill of bean sprouts. As we speak, Gwyn's immaculate poop chute probably has a few apple peels, a bite of celery, and maybe a couple pomegranate seeds stuck in it, whereas a normal person's colon houses up to 10 pounds of sludge, comprised of partially digested hamburger, pepperoni, green peppers and onions, cheese fries, Speculoos Cookie Butter, and an Egg McMuffin or two.

The aforementioned substances, when they have hardened, ***are not easy*** to dislodge from the intestinal walls. Believe me, a quart of prune-broccoli-kale-carrot juice won't cut it. What us snackers need are small rectal plungers, with soft rubber heads and fail-safe wooden handles without splinters.

Sadly, we can't trust our Chinese masters to provide these delicate butt-plunging instruments, what with their inability to manufacture a screw that doesn't break off in a pre-drilled hole. But as I said, the juicing option is even less attractive for weight management, and the chubby **must not be forced** to ingest liquid foodstuffs that normal human beings (not Gwyneth Paltrow) may find sickeningly repulsive (Gwyneth Paltrow).

CHAPTER 8

OPRAH'S FEET

Since you did so well making the connection between Amy Schumer's panties and body image, you shouldn't have any trouble figuring out how Oprah's feet fit into the picture. *OMG, I just realized how hilarious "fit into the picture" is going to strike you in a minute or two. Letterman should have picked me to replace him instead of Stephen Colbert. Nothing against Colbert. He's hotter than Sriracha sauce, except for that one hideously deformed ear. I had to get out the bottle to see how to spell that sauce. WTF? That's some weird spelling shit there.*

Anyways, with diets and juicing off the table (*off the table ha ha*) we started to search for other remedies, perhaps something that wasn't quite as drastic as having to eat vegetables and drink juice. That's where Oprah comes in. Realistically, it's just not possible to get through a discourse on weight loss without Oprah munching and chomping her way onto the scene.

I'm getting a little annoyed at having to defend my highly nuanced constructive criticisms by pandering to my readers' blind devotion to their favorite celebrities. I LOVE OPRAH TOO, OK? BUT SHE IS/WAS/MAY AGAIN BE FAT, OK? AND BEING FAT IS OK, OK? If you can't stand the heat, get out of the kitchen, my friend. But don't let Oprah's ass hit you on the way out. I'm fairly certain Oprah would find all this extremely funny, because she's like Jesus, very humble and good-natured, only a lot richer and bulkier.

If I had Oprah's money, I'd eat anything and everything I wanted in huge quantities, and then I'd hire the best photoshoppers money could buy to make me look thin in my photographs, and the other people in the photographs look much fatter, even if they were the size of manatees to begin with. Maybe Oprah's already done that. I noticed in a recent issue of **O Magazine** that she was on the cover, looking gorgeously svelte, in the middle of a group of women so … **substantial** … they appeared to have gobbled themselves all the way from plus-size to plorse-size in one sitting.

The last time I saw a photo of Oprah's best friend, Gayle King, she was looking kind of hefty too, whereas Oprah looked like she'd shaved off a ton, or had hired someone with killer graphic skills to shave it off for her. And one final observation about Oprah's photoshoppers. On another cover of **O Magazine**, she's sitting outdoors, in a workout suit, with a purple shawl ingeniously draped over her bulging sidecars. Something caught my attention about this glossy cover, and it wasn't that Oprah looked, as she always does on O's covers, as though she'd just come from an hour at the gym, where she'd shed 20 pounds on the massage table. It was her right foot I zeroed in on.

The foot looked fake. In fact, it looked like a wooden foot, the kind you might see someplace that sells wooden feet. The painted-on toes were tiny, and more or less carved in a straight line. I got out a magnifying glass and studied the foot more closely. Something definitely wasn't right about it. It wasn't in proportion to the rest of Oprah's body, and didn't look like it could support a woman of her stature. I called my old man, an expert in all things feet, over to have a look. "What the hell's wrong with Oprah's foot in this picture? Has she had foot reduction surgery, or is this thing bogus?"

"It looks like Oprah's foot has really slimmed down," he said. "The rest of her is still kind of tubby, but that foot could be a contestant on The Biggest Loser." I never can rely on my old man to give me his honest opinion of Oprah. It's because I love her so much, and won't tolerate even the slightest hint of criticism of her in my presence. My old man knows if he fucks up and says the wrong thing about Oprah, I'll clean the dogs' paws with his toothbrush again. In fact, I love Oprah so much that I once wrote her a letter, offering to replace Gayle King as her best friend.

Dear Oprah,

If you accept me instead of Gayle as your new BFF, I guarantee you won't have to waste thousands of dollars buying me shit from your "Favorite Things" list, like that $100 orange tee shirt with "You Go, Girl" on it that I'd just end up throwing in the Goodwill bag or passing on to my sister-in-law. And you won't have to set up college funds for my kids either, because I don't have any kids. I am blessed with dog children, as you are, Oprah. And one of my kids is black, like you.

And by the way, Oprah, I will take care of your precious dog children whenever you travel, and if, by chance, anything happened to you, I would adopt them and raise them as my own, and not have them put to sleep as a woman with a busy TV network career might, after telling everybody your precious babies would be better off dead because they were mourning for you and pissing up and down the walls of her fancy schmancy penthouse apartment in NYC.

Oprah, God as my judge, as your new best friend, I swear I will never ever accuse Stedman or yourself of being secretly gay, no matter what I see going on behind closed doors in any of your mansions, and even if I do see something unseemly going on, or if Stedman (or yourself) puts the make on me or my old man, my lips will be sealed forever. And Oprah, I will never, even if water boarded by Cheney himself, reveal your true weight.

Love always from your most adoring fan,
Ellen Garrison

I never received a reply, but with Gayle packing on the pounds like she is, I'm sure I'll be in the running if Oprah decides to dump her. The point I'm getting at is that I worship Oprah so damn much, I let her talk me into joining Weight Watchers. As a spokeswoman for WW, she began encouraging her acolytes to join up and experience WW's new program, which had a revised points system that included subtracting points for exercise. Sounded great.

The best part was that Oprah would be losing weight right along with us, offering encouragement and weight loss tips in the pages of *O Magazine*. How could we go wrong? Using my old man's debit card, I went online and signed us both up. As long as I had his card number, I went ahead and ordered a WW cookbook, WW food scale, and WW points calculator.

Then I went to Amazon and ordered a fold-up stationary bike, two yoga mats, stretchy exercise bands and wrist weights. A little concerned that I might inadvertently miss out on Oprah's guidance and counsel, I used the card to extend my subscription to *O Magazine* by two years. Then I sat back, ready to watch the pounds melt away.

"Jesus Mary and Joe Fucking Biden," my old man exploded when he saw all the debit card transactions on his credit union statement. "What the hell is all this?"

"You need to lose a ton of weight," I told him bluntly, "…or you're going to grow another hernia from packing that big gut around. I've ordered some things that will help you do that, and I'm even going to suffer along with you. It's for your own sake, and for the sake of the boys. They need you alive and earning money to pay for their premium dog food and granola treats."

"Looks more like it's for the good of Weight Watchers and *O Magazine*, if you ask me," my old man said, unaware he was treading on dangerous ground. "We both could have had liposuction for what you spent on this stuff."

"You know, that sounds a little like an Oprah dig," I said, a note of caution entering my voice. My old man immediately backed off.

"Whatever…" he said resignedly. "I'm not going up against Oprah again. Cleaning the boys' feet with my toothbrush was maybe one of the shittiest things you've ever done." I had to agree with him on that, but sometimes the punishment has to fit the crime, and this was Oprah we were talking about.

The day after I set up our accounts, I started receiving a slew of emails from Weight Watchers requesting that I send them our food and exercise profiles, food preferences, etc. I complied, and in return received what was to be our daily point total limits. Based on what I'd put in, my old man's limit was going to be 32 points each day for his food and beverages, with allowances for more points, depending on the amount of time he spent exercising. My point total limit was 60 points per day. I was quite pleased with this algorithm, but my old man clearly was not.

"Son of a bitch," he bleated. "Why do I only get 32 lousy points and you get 60?"

"Because I'm going to be more active than you," I snapped. "While you sit on your fat ass all day, I'm going to be averaging 50 miles on the stationary bike, doing Pilates and pumping iron with my wrist weights. I'm going to be burning calories out the wazoo."

"Wait a minute," he said suspiciously. "How much weight did you tell them I needed lose?"

"Well, I sort of combined our numbers," I admitted. "I was thinking you need to lose around 100 pounds, and I could use to take off maybe 20. So I rounded it up to 120 pounds total and put that on your form." He shook his head and reached for the wine box. "Go easy on that," I cautioned. "…at least until we figure out the points in 16 ounces of merlot."

The news wasn't good. My old man investigated WW's website and deduced that **all** of our daily point totals were going to be used up in alcohol consumption alone, and that he was going to start running a huge deficit by the end of the first day of the program.

We were also not impressed by WW's discrimination against some of our favorite foods. They had an absolute case of the ass against anything that came off a hog, and bacon was a major no-no. Turkey bacon didn't generate quite as much disapproval as real bacon, but who the hell is going to settle for turkey on a bacon cheeseburger or on a BLT with extra mayo?

Most of our usual snack foods were banned in favor of cut up vegetables and non-fat dips, and peanut butter was second only to the despised bacon. Unless we could think of some way to completely alter their unreasonable point system, this Weight Watchers gig was going to be a lot harder than I'd thought.

The food scale and the points calculator arrived by the end of the following week. I couldn't figure out how to use the calculator, so I put it back in the box and stored it in my "gifts" bin. My old man's sister was a lot savvier about these modern gadgets than I was. She'd know how to use it.

The food scale was tiny, with a small detachable container on top that couldn't hold more than a fistful of potato chips at best. I tried to calibrate the thing by loading it with Cheetos, but its flimsy box fell off onto the floor, and the boys swarmed around my feet, jockeying for access to the tasty snacks. I tried to hold them back with the toe of my shoe, but lost my balance and stepped on the plastic container, smashing it to smithereens. This wasn't going well at all. I angrily stuffed the scale and fragments of the plastic container back in the box. It was a total loss, and now I had two hyper dogs with orange muzzles.

When the stationary bike arrived, my old man put it together in about 20 minutes. I climbed onto the apparatus and pedaled a mile or so before deciding that the seat was extraordinarily rigid and uncomfortable. How the hell was I supposed to do 50 miles a day on the contraption without setting my ass on fire? I dismounted, and went to the computer to order a padded saddle. The damn things were $25! I contemplated removing bicycling from my list of point-increasing activities, but then my wine consumption would suffer.

What kind of hellish situation had I gotten myself into? There wasn't room in the trailer to store the bicycle (unfolded) so that it would be convenient for me to use every day. I decided it would have to sit outside. Maybe I could find a spot for it beside the barbeque grill. But what if it rained? How was I going to get it up the steps and into the trailer without getting wet? I priced small portable shells used for motorcycles. The cheapest was $325 + shipping. This weight loss plan was getting totally out of hand.

The stretchy exercise bands and wrist weights were no problem at all. I shoved them in a low cabinet and closed the door. It swung back open. Getting down on hands and knees, I reached into the back of the cabinet to see what was preventing the door from shutting all the way, and my hand closed around a 5 pound dumbbell. There was another beside it. Damn! I'd forgotten I put them in there when we'd moved.

They'd never been used, so theoretically they could be added to the future gift bin. On the other hand, it would cost a fortune to mail the goddamn things all the way to Seattle.

In the meantime, I was getting more emails from Weight Watchers, pressuring me to tell them what I'd been up to, what I'd been eating and how much I'd been exercising. To be honest, I was getting a little tired of them prying into my eating and drinking habits. It was really none of their goddamn business. I thumbed through their spiral bound, $22 cookbook, and couldn't find but about 3 recipes that looked palatable. All three were desserts. I hunted in vain for good recipes with bacon as the main ingredient. There were none.

My disillusionment was complete when my old man explained the points system's algorithm to me in detail. Not being a math expert, I forget what all he said, except for the part about cutting down on macaroni and cheese, and drinking one serving of wine per day from a shot glass instead of a Big Gulp cup. Clearly, this Weight Watchers program wasn't going to succeed for my old man. He didn't have the self-discipline I did, and I wasn't about to put up with this kind of enforced moderation if it didn't work for the both of us.

When they were about to expire, I cancelled our WW memberships. They wanted to know why I wasn't renewing, and I told them that their program didn't work. Neither me nor my old man had lost one pound. In fact, we'd both gained a pound or two, binge eating while we fretted over the program's dismal failure. We took the stationary bike over to our storage unit, where it now sits beside the other stationary bike I forgot I already had. We may sell them both on Craigslist.

The WW cookbook went into the future gift bin along with the calculator. They'll make thoughtful gifts for my sister-in-law. I'm still planning on using the stretchy bands and wrist weights one of these days, and when I do, I'm going to need the yoga mats I bought and put away somewhere. If I can't find them, I may have to buy two more. Even though WW didn't work out for us, it still saved me a lot of traipsing around, looking for Christmas presents.

And Oprah, if you're out there reading my book and want to recommend **Trailer Dogs** to your Book Club peeps, go right ahead. You have my blessing.

After all, what are best friends for?

CHAPTER 9

TRAILER DOGS: THE MOVIE

It's a Mad Mad Mad Mad Dog World

I have always been a live and let live person. I do not enjoy confrontation on any level, except maybe when a manufacturer sends me a coupon for a free case of dog food after I write them a nasty letter accusing them of trying to poison my boys with their new formula.

And then there was the other time when I got mad at the makers of Easy-On spray starch because their can nozzle always clogged up, and I wrote them and suggested they change the name of their product to Hard-On spray starch. They sent me a bunch of coupons for free starch, which was a complete waste, because by then I was too lazy to iron anything and was buying only Permanent Press stuff.

I'm not a complainer. I hardly ever send food back in a restaurant, even when they fuck up at McDonald's and put slop on my Big Mac when I didn't order it that way. In that case, I usually put on my woman pants and make my old man eat the burger while I take his McNuggets. I am not a trouble maker, and I abhor physical violence of any type. I will discipline neither dog nor human child, regardless of how many times they piss on the leg of my sofa or gnar the fringe off my antique Kilim rug.

People close to me will tell you that I'm not judgmental, vindictive or even sarcastic - unless, of course, circumstances demand that I step in and call a spade a spade. I don't resort to name-calling if there's any way around it.

In fact, Dear Reader, if you've managed to rouse yourself from the mindless stupor you were in at the beginning of **Trailer Dogs**, you may recall how furious I was at that writer who threatened to punch me in the throat for treating my dogs like they were my children. But instead of wrestling her malicious carcass down into the gutter and wringing her scrawny neck as many less mild-tempered people would have done, I set my anger aside, and turned negativity into positivity by writing a book. Hopefully, the success of **Trailer Dogs** will shame and humiliate her enough so that she will never again publicly threaten me or my dogs. It's called **turning the other cheek**, and it's in the Bible.

I am a serene individual, and will go far out of my way to avoid conflict. That said, me and my old man recently got into a knock-down drag-out fight that lasted almost 48 hours. It was over the casting of **Trailer Dogs: The Movie**.

The evening started out pleasantly enough, with a full box of merlot, two sheets of paper and two pens. The object of our planning exercise was that each of us would write down who we thought could best play the characters in **Trailer Dogs: The Movie**. We began with the less important dramatis personae.

Author's Note: Again, you'll have to look up the definition of dramatis personae for yourselves. I probably shouldn't have used that term. The Kardashians may buy my book, and we all know what a bunch of dopes they are, except for Caitlyn.

My original suggestion for the unpleasant, disagreeable Resort manager, Gretchen, was Carly Fiorina (costumed in a fat suit). Even though Fiorina is slightly younger and more attractive than Gretchen, and is not even an actress, I thought she would bring to the role exactly the unpleasant, sanctimonious, sourpuss, malicious characteristics needed to pull it off. My old man was so receptive to my excellent casting idea, he actually crossed out the two candidates he'd written down.

That decision made, we proceeded to

Excuse me a sec, folks, but I just detected a long hair growing out the side of my neck. I need to go pluck it out before I forget. brb Wow, that really fucking hurt! One time somebody told me that stray hairs on an old person's chin can grow up to 5 or 6 inches in a couple days. No wonder they're so crabby and in a bad mood if they have to put up with that kind of shit. Note to self: Be more tolerant of and kind to Geezers in the future.

Anyway, as I was saying, the part of Gretchen decided, we moved on to casting the roles of Lulu the Bichon and her Trailer Dog Dad, Gerald. Once again my old man deferred to my superior judgment in proposing David Carradine for the role of Gerald. Carradine, as the quirky, unpredictable Gerald, was perfect in every way for the part. And as an added bonus, I figured we could probably get Carradine cheap since I hadn't seen him in any movies in a long time.

Casting Lulu the Bichon was more problematic, what with her unfortunate size. The little dog was massively overweight, and it was going to be tough finding a double for her (no pun intended) among the canine actors in Hollywood. I wondered if maybe we should call the agent who represented Arnold (the pig) from Green Acres to see if he would be available for an audition, assuming the pig was still alive after all these years, and that his trainer could get him accustomed to wearing a fat suit. We agreed that ***Trailer Dogs'*** costume designer was going to have his/her hands full just stitching up all the fat suits we were going to need.

Ben and Sully, of course, would play themselves in the movie. They would be highly paid for their performances, as would their Trainer/Manager. And who better to supervise Ben and Sully during filming than myself, their Guardian and protector?

I could be on the set day and night, instructing the director about the boys' performances. All we'd need was a small trailer in which they could practice their scenes, and where I could retreat to develop any additional dialog that I felt would improve and enhance their roles.

In fact, now that I thought about it, I could perform this management task for the entire cast. The added responsibility would require a much higher salary, naturally, and the film's backers would have to furnish me with a 35 to 40-foot RV, equipped with the proper electronics and communications devices, a stocked refrigerator, and possibly an on-site masseuse, seeing as how I would be extremely tense after a long day's shoot.

We were zooming right along with my fantastic casting and production ideas, when around 11 pm, the wine box ran dry and things started to go south in short order. I had written down "Jennifer Garner" as the actress I was certain had the chops to play myself in

Trailer Dogs: The Movie. Garner clearly had everything the role demanded - youthful good looks, warmth, dimpled charm, charisma, - you name it. And the actress was long overdue a nod from Academy Awards idiots who, incredibly, had overlooked her brilliant performance in ***Catch and Release.*** Despite the poor woman's unfortunate divorce from the giant-headed Ben Affleck (Garner should have known better than to marry a man with a head that abnormally gargantuan) I knew she'd be ideal to play me in ***Trailer Dogs.***

For unknown reasons (possibly related to the bone dry wine box), my old man took exception to Jennifer Garner as my movie doppelganger. The agreeable, obliging spouse who'd just minutes before extolled as sheer genius my casting of David Carradine as Gerald, instantly turned into the abusive, loathsome monster that was always lurking just below the surface of his "Mr. Nice Guy" facade. "Don't you think Jennifer Garner is a little too young to play you?" he muttered, his voice dripping with sarcasm and contempt.

"Don't you think you're a little too much of a big asshole?" I responded, answering him in kind. "I guess you have a better idea who to cast as me than me. Let's see what you wrote down there." Somewhat hesitantly, he handed me his notepaper. In a mocking, sadistic scrawl he had written "Kathy Bates."

"I knew it!" I spat. "This is just like you to sit there and throw a poison turd in my face and insult me like that. You want Kathy Bates because you think I'm like her character in ***Misery***," I said, swinging a wooden back scratcher in his general direction. "All that crazy ass 'mister man' shit and whacking James Caen's knees with a mallet ... her character was a fucking psycho!"

"I'm not insulting you or implying you're a psycho," my old man backpedaled, cautiously trying to exit the minefield he'd created for himself. "Kathy Bates is a fantastic actress. She's not bad looking. She can play anybody. I just think she's more age-appropriate."

The last time someone had used the term "age appropriate" on me was when I'd asked for blonde highlights and my hair colorist suggested I might want to go with something a "little more age appropriate." "Well, what about some purple and orange streaks like the ones you have in **your** fucking hair," I shot back. "Maybe that'll go over better for me down at the goddamn old folks' home." She shut her trap and got out the bleach.

My old man wasn't finished with his push for Kathy Bates. "And ... boy ... the ... way," he added, enunciating each word as though he was Bernie Sanders lecturing Jesus on a more equitable method for distributing loaves and fishes, "In case you forgot, Kathy Bates won an Oscar for her performance in **Misery**."

By then it was almost 1 am. I'd been awake since 10 that morning and had worked on the book most of the day. The boys had long since hustled off to bed, and were curled up on our pillows, snoring, or in Sully's case, growling, peacefully. It seemed like a good time to ignore the horrific verbal abuse I'd just experienced, let bygones be bygones, and take up the casting of **Trailer Dogs: The Movie** the next evening after we were rested and had a chance to re-stock our box wine reserves.

"Well…" I said, wearily, "I don't give two shits whether Bates won an Oscar or not. She's **not** playing me in *Trailer Dogs.* Jennifer Garner's getting the part and that's all there is to it."

"And…by … the…way," I added, "I'm tapping John Goodman for **your** part. The special effects team will have to create a mask to make him look older and jowlier – if that's even possible - but we'll just have to suck up the extra expense on that one."

"Holy shit, you're waaaay over-reacting," my old man exclaimed through his detestable blowhole, repeating a phrase he dredges up every time he makes some bombastic, hateful remark he wishes he could retract before I have a chance to respond. "John Goodman is a fine actor, and he's wonderful in everything he does. I'm just kind of surprised you didn't think of Jeff Bridges to play me."

There it was. The **real** reason for my old man's incredible disregard for his own well-being. He was interfering with **my** casting decisions, and trying to finagle Jeff Bridges into **my** movie. I should have known he'd become tyrannical and domineering about this. He'd had a "thing" for Bridges ever since *The Big Lebowski*. It was pathetic in a way -- to see him debase and humiliate himself over a one-sided bro-mance with "The Dude." Not wanting him to embarrass himself any further, I tried to let him down gently.

"You have got to be fucking kidding me," I said, burying my face in my hands. "If you think for one second an actor of Jeff Bridges' caliber would accept a boring, dead-end part in a blockbuster film like *Trailer Dogs*, you've lost your fucking mind. Besides, I doubt he'd be willing to shave his beard and wear an old person mask just to come up empty-handed while Jennifer Garner snags the Oscar. But if John Goodman isn't to your liking, maybe I'll offer the part to that guy who plays Gloria's husband on **Modern Family**." I suggested this in a bona fide effort to guide my old man to an easy escape route from the lion's den he'd carelessly wandered into.

He looked perplexed. "You mean Ed O'Neill..?"

"Yup. If I can get Ed O'Neill to play you, we won't have to worry about using an old person mask or maybe even a fat suit," I said, driving my point home. "And O'Neill's going to be looking for work soon enough. **Modern Family's** been slipping in the ratings ever since its gay fans realized the handsome dude who plays Phil Dunphy isn't one of them."

Around 3 in the morning we declared a truce after my old man gave in and admitted that Jennifer Garner was indeed the only actress with the looks and cred to play me in **Trailer Dogs: The Movie**. He also came around to my picks for the rest of the cast, most of whom were older actors and actresses I hoped would still be alive by the time we started filming. We could work out the details later, including my plan for getting Joel and Ethan Coen to direct. With heavyweights like them in the loop, maybe Billy Bob Thornton would come on board. I was sure we could find a spot for him in the cast, even if I had to add a touching homicidal psychopath like Sling Blade to the script at the last minute.

To show good faith to my old man, I stopped pressing for John Goodman to play his part. I hadn't really been all that sold on Goodman in the first place, and since he's lost a lot of weight recently, he would have unquestionably needed a fat suit. All those fat suits were threatening to become a real drain on the film's budget.

The truth was, I'd set my heart on Kevin Spacey to play my old man. I've worshiped Spacey ever since **LA Confidential** when he was the jaded detective who, with his dying breath, uttered "Rollo Tomasi," setting up that old geezer who played the corrupt, murderous police captain, and who was also the farmer who owned the brainy talking pig in the movie, **Babe**. Even though I was exhausted and longing for sleep, that gave me another brilliant thought: If Arnold from **Green Acres** was dead, or was unavailable due to other contract commitments, we could get that **Babe** pig to play Lulu the Bichon. If memory served, the **Babe** pig was a much more versatile performer than Arnold the Pig, and was also plumper. Maybe we could forego another fat suit.

As I made the remainder of the casting choices for **Trailer Dogs**, it occurred to me that it might be a bit of a problem getting Kevin Spacey signed. He was, after all, starring in the hit TV series **House of Cards**, where he was playing the half-gay President of the United States, Frank Underwood. There again, I marveled at the breadth of the man's acting ability.

One memorable scene in **House of Cards** had required Spacey to join in a threesome with his "wife," the irresistibly handsome, broad-shouldered Lesbian actress Robin Wright, and a male secret service agent. Spacey had acted the difficult part as though he might have written it for himself. It made me desire him all the more. No wonder my old man was jealous of my motives in tapping Spacey to play him in

Trailer Dogs: The Movie. Undoubtedly we'd run into each other on the set, and in Hollywood, anything can happen.

The next night, armed with fresh boxes of wine, and having slept almost 16 hours straight, I completed the final-final casting decisions for ***Trailer Dogs: The Movie***, and passed the list to my old man. After perusing it for about 2 minutes, he handed it back to me and shrugged. "Whatever…"

Always the peacemaker, I let him have the last word.

ELLEN GARRISON

TRAILER DOGS CAST OF CHARACTERS
&
COSTUME REQUIREMENTS

Ellen Garrison:	Jennifer Garner (Understudy: Sofia Vergara)
My Old Man:	Kevin Spacey (2 fat suits will be required unless Mike Myers still has his Fat Bastard costume from *Austin Powers* and will lend it to us.)
Ben & Sully:	As Themselves (No fat suits will be required)
Gretchen Bird:	Carly Fiorina (fat suit)
Lloyd Bird:	William F. Macy (Spanx body suit will be required to slenderize Macy)
Charles Bird:	Carly Fiorina's dog (fat suit)
Lonnie May:	Bill Murray
Daisy May:	Claymation figure (fat suit)
Gerald Karn:	David Carradine
Lulu Karn:	Pig from *Babe* (fat suit may be needed)
Ian Reeve:	William Shatner
Ian's Wife:	Caitlyn Jenner
Virginia Lopp:	Betty White (fat suit)
Claudia:	Amy Schumer (fat suit)
Laurette:	Kirstie Alley (fat suit)

TRAILER DOGS CAST OF CHARACTERS
&
COSTUME REQUIREMENTS, CONT.

Cripple Jon:	Billy Bob Thornton
Marv Greer:	Ed O'Neill (fat suit)
Patty Greer:	Kathy Bates (fat suit)
Bill Crane:	Robert DeNiro
Phyllis Crane:	Jane Fonda
Church Lady & Husband.:	Tracey Ullman (dual role) (fat suit) (fat suit)
Oprah Winfrey:	Herself (fat suit to be determined)

CHAPTER 10

MY OLD MAN

I realize that in the warning at the beginning of ***Trailer Dogs***, I may have said that the book was, to sort of quote me, "almost pure fiction." ***There's no need for you to go back and check on this. You'd just be wasting your time and mine.***

As it turns out, that statement is only partly true. Truth, as I've come to believe, comes in many forms, including bald-faced lies. But sometimes, the whole, unadulterated truth must be told, regardless of how much it may piss somebody off, namely me. My old man, who I'd like to call George Clooney (if Clooney hadn't gone off and married that Elvira woman), is the one who pisses me off. The. Most.

What you are about to read is heavily based on facts, and consists of things my old man has done or is still doing that would infuriate the Prince of Peace himself, and which, in fact, may be the reason The Second Coming has been so long delayed.

As shameful and embarrassing as it would be to a normal person, my airing of his dirty laundry won't bother my old man in the least, because he thinks a tell-all about him will sell more books, and he also still thinks he's getting 20% of the profits. I could write that he's a big fat crooked ape-turd and a lying asshole loser, and he'd ignore the slights because of that imaginary 20%. How dumb is that? Kinda reminds me of Chris Christie. Also, and I can't explain this without access to proper mind-expanding pharmaceuticals, my old man is actually *proud* of all the shit he pulls.

I worry (well, not really, to be even more truthful with you) that by now, many of you may have a false impression that my old man is some kind of martyr, and that I'm profane, too quick to anger, ill-tempered, judgmental, and prone to making snide, knife-twisting comments about those who rub me the wrong way.

Oh, and vindictive. I almost forgot that one. I'm really not all that concerned about what readers think of me behind my back, because a lot of people have said these same untrue, hurtful things to my face, and they've known me a hell of a lot longer than you have. What none of you seem to have picked up on in your rush to judgment is the clear and simple fact that: **For years, my old man has been trying to kill me.**

"You're being paranoid." I know that's what you people are thinking. I hear the phrase time and time again from my old man when he's trying to compensate for a stupifyingly dumb remark he just made. He also says that when he's made a questionable observation about me to someone that I found out about by secretly listening in on his phone conversations.

Like last December around Christmas. I'd come into the room after I heard my name mentioned during a phone conversation he was having with his sister. He looked right at me and stopped talking. God knows what crap he'd been filling her with, but I heard the word "gift" mentioned.

He was probably telling her that I flushed the hand-made sequined butterfly magnets she'd sent me for my birthday down the toilet and plugged up the black water tank in the process. To make the incident (and me) look worse, he would have left out the mitigating circumstances in which I'd first pureed the monstrosities in a blender so they'd fit down the drain. Judge my behavior as you will, but you wouldn't have wanted those fucking eyesores on your fridge either.

There is no doubt in my mind that every time my old man and his sister talk on the phone, they cluck like two old hens about me and my so-called "paranoia." Now that I think about it, she might be in on his plot to kill me. She hasn't approved of me since I let her 6-year old son and his older brother stay up late and watch **Boyz n the Hood** when they slept over at our house one weekend 30 years ago. She acted like it was all my fault, as if I should have known the kids were lying when they said they were allowed to watch R-rated movies any goddamn time they wanted. And then she turned around and blamed *me* when they called their grandmother an "old white ho" to her face.

I get sick and tired of my old man trying to convince people that *I'm* the bad one in our relationship, and claiming that I'm being paranoid when I expose his plans to do away with me. I've lost count of the times his attempts on my life have failed. There was the time in Seattle when I was helping him make repairs to our patio roof, and he "accidentally" dropped a 2 X 8 on my head. Then there was the day when he was reefing the sail on our small sailboat and "accidentally" dropped the boom on my head. When we were helping a neighbor finish constructing his mountain cabin, my old man "accidentally" dropped a log on my head.

Not long ago he was reaching for a box of bed slats in our storage unit, and it "accidentally" slipped from his grasp and fell on my head. Then there was the time I didn't cook salmon fillets long enough, and we both got food poisoning. He whined that he was too sick to drive me to the ER. And how could I forget last week, when I woke up and he was trying to smother me with a bed pillow? He didn't even **try** to explain *that* shit away. He's getting more brazen all the time.

What makes me even madder than my old man plotting to kill me, is how nonchalantly he insults my intelligence by lying about it. If he'd just admit to the conspiracies and treachery, I think maybe I could live with it. It's like Bill tells Hillary about interns and flight attendants: "Who are you going to believe, me or your own two eyes?" My situation is a little different than Hillary Clinton's. While I don't trust my eyes because my vision isn't worth a crap, I do believe what I think I heard with my own two ears. **Note to self: You might want to re-write this part just in case you-know-who is elected President and starts snooping your emails again.**

To those of you who have gone behind my back to gossip with your friends about whether or not I'm paranoid: I don't appreciate it. Your duplicity prevents me from pinning down my detractors with irrefutable evidence, like OJ's DNA slathered all over everything at the scene of the murder. And it makes me feel like I did when I was twelve, and overheard my mom comforting her sister, Mary. Aunt Mary was distraught over my cousin, James, who been hospitalized after he was kicked in the head by a neighbor's horse. James was 42, unmarried, unemployed, and living at home at the time.

When the unfortunate accident occurred, James apparently had been trying to force himself sexually on the agitated filly. There was no solid proof of felonious intent, either on the part of James or the horse, other than when they found him, James' pants were down around his ankles, and his forehead had an appalling crater in it in the shape of a horseshoe.

That James was weird was well known to all of us, even before he was assaulted by the horse. When we went to visit Aunt Mary and Uncle Al, as we often did, James was either holed up in his attic bedroom, "working on his hobbies" as Aunt Mary explained, or off somewhere in one of the barns or pastures near their farm. Later, as we were hugging and kissing Aunt Mary and Uncle Al goodbye, we'd see James lurking in the shadows behind the trees along the driveway, waiting until we drove away.

Mom explained James' antisocial inclinations by saying that he was just "too painfully shy" to express his affection for us. "James was a 'premie'" Mom reasoned, as if to justify his loopy behavior. "He was born without a hymen membrane – like the Kennedy baby."

Being a JFK admirer and somewhat of an expert on all things Kennedy, I figured Mom was confused with the "hyaline membrane disease" that had killed Jack and Jackie's premature infant, but I wasn't ready to let James off the hook. It seemed to me more likely that James spied on us from the far fringes of the driveway to make sure we were actually leaving. It was hard to tell from that distance, but he seemed pleased, in a sinister sort of way, that he could get back to his attic hideaway, or whatever it was he was up to in the neighbor's horse barn, without having to interact with his relatives.

"The psychiatrist says Jamie needs help, that he's schizophrenic," I heard Aunt Mary tearfully confide to Mom after the horse incident. "But *I'm his mother,* and I *know* Jamie isn't schizophrenic. It's just…from time to time he hears voices inside his head, ordering him to do sinful things."

"Well, Mare," Mom commiserated, using the nickname her sister had since they were kids. (and which, in retrospect, seems ironic), "This feels to me like it might be the work of Satan. Jamie hasn't been blaspheming has he?"

Mare blew air out her nostrils and shook her mane in vigorous denial. "Jamie blaspheme?" she said, recoiling in horror. "**Of course not!** Jamie's been a good Christian his whole life. He was saved by Jesus when he was only seven. The boy never even uses swear words." she added forcefully.

While I had the utmost respect for and sympathy with my beloved and sweet-as-peaches Aunt Mary, I possessed contradictory information as to James' use of profanity. Once, when a female cousin and I visited Aunt Mary without our moms, James, sweaty after a lengthy trip to the horse pasture, cornered us in the hallway. "What are you two sneaky cunts up to?" he hissed at us, "You filthy little whores better keep away from my room if you know what's good for you."

My cousin, DeDe, who didn't take crap off anybody, even adults like James, looked him right in the eye. "Fuck you, perv," she tossed over her shoulder as she barreled past him in the hall. Emboldened by

DeDe's assertiveness, I chimed in. "Yeah, nobody wants to go in your creepy old room. It smells like horseshit in there."

Uh oh. How would I know that James' room was creepy and smelled like horseshit unless I'd been in there? How would I know the scratches on his door lock came from DeDe's pen knife? Either James failed to make the connection, or he was in such a hurry to get back to his bedroom that he paid no attention to what either one of us said. Or maybe it *was* just voices inside his head ordering James to call his twelve year old girl cousins "cunts" and "whores," and not the work of Satan.

At least that's what Aunt Mary continued to believe after James was committed to the state mental hospital. He had a nice room on the third floor, a picture of Black Beauty hanging on the wall over his cot, and when Aunt Mary visited him, she brought along his favorite carrot cake and oatmeal cookies. James might have been schizophrenic and a sociopath, but nobody ever stooped so low as to call him paranoid, like my old man does me behind my back.

My old man has a super high IQ. It's so high, in fact, that at first glance you might not realize that although he wasn't born into Trailer Dog culture, he's embraced it with the same intensity and enthusiasm Anthony Wiener reserves for his wiener. When we built our first house back in the 90s, my old man bought a book and taught himself how to do the electrical wiring. He did all the plumbing too, again, learning how from books on the subject. Everything was done up to building codes, and his work passed muster with county and state inspectors.

He can fix just about anything mechanical if he has a roll of duct tape and Gorilla glue. He knows how to install most any type of electronic equipment, and he makes a living developing computer systems that can process credit cards and payrolls in the blink of an eye, or predict with a high degree of certainty where the next catastrophic earthquake is going to be centered.

There are many, many, many, many, many, many things my old man *can't* fix, however, and subjects he knows zilch about. I dare not bring this up unless I am prepared to endure marathon pouting. And to be completely honest, a lot of the things my old man has to fix are things he broke fixing something else. This is what can cause a person to start having dreams about chewing her husband's face off … like the kind Patty Greer has about Marv.

Being as smart as he is, one would think my old man might be able to button his shirt correctly two days in a row and remember where we've stored toilet paper for the last year and a half. One might also rightfully assume that a guy who scored so well on his SATs and received so many scholarship offers from some of the best colleges and universities in the US, would also know how to fill an ice cube tray without spilling the water over every fucking surface inside and outside the refrigerator, so much so that ice cubes come out the size of peas.

And speaking of refrigerators, here's something that happened JUST TODAY. The cold-sensing mechanism inside our RV fridge got yanked loose – by my old man - when he was fixing something else in there. He was half-baked at the time of the repairs, and probably thought he was reaching for a can of beer.

Anyways, he patched things up enough so nothing would thaw out overnight, and he said the first thing this morning he would call the RV dealer for advice on how to put things right in the fridge. I talked to him at noon today and asked if he'd called the RV repair guys yet. He said no, that they would be super busy, and that he didn't want to bother them over the phone. Then he went on to say that he was going to stop by the RV place this afternoon, in person, and ask them how to fix the fridge. In my old man's deranged mind, he thinks he's ***being more considerate by aggravating people in person than aggravating them on the phone.***

When we first started dating, I overlooked his terrible faults, - like his passionate, insatiable interest in physics, math and sexual intercourse. I dealt with his reprehensible shortcomings like the shrewd teenager I was, feigning interest in his pursuits in order to get him to do my homework. The algebra and chemistry parts were particularly difficult to wrap my legs around, but my old man didn't seem to mind the extra tutoring sessions.

Later, when we got married, my mother-in-law sat me down and briefed me on how to care for her brilliant, but preoccupied son. "Don't expect too much from him," she cautioned "He's a big thinker, and he's going to have too much on his mind to care about your day-to-day problems, or to be helpful and supportive of you all the time." As it turned out, she was spot-on in her prediction. But my own grandmother, a woman who'd been widowed five times, had some marital advice of her own:

"Always keep your windowsills dusted, honey," she counseled, "And have a nice hot meal waiting for him when he gets home from his job. But if he so much as looks at another woman, you come back here, and Granny will give you her recipe for poison mushroom soup." I was pretty sure Nana was joking about the mushroom soup, but then again, her windowsills were always spotless and yet she'd racked up five dead husbands, all of them philanderers and soup eaters.

When he was growing up, my old man was called "The Beaver," and not because he had buck teeth or resembled the child actor, Jerry Mathers (if the producers of Leave it to Beaver had dressed Mathers in a fat suit). My old man earned the Beaver handle because he tampered with every appliance and electronic device that came into the house. When his Mom pulled out the Hoover to vacuum, she'd find the motor had been removed. Same thing with all the radios and TVs. When the insides of any gadget went missing, The Beaver was always the first suspect they dragged in for questioning.

"Beaver, beaver, beaver," my mother-in-law sighed, as she reminisced about the time she and my father-in-law were planning a trip to The Big Apple. She'd gone out and bought a pricey little travel percolator to take along on the trip. ***This was back in the day when even the finest hotels didn't equip rooms with miniature Mr. Coffees, and room service was a pain in the ass for serious caffeine addicts like her.***

When they decamped in the hotel room, the first thing she unpacked was the new percolator, still in its fine leather case. As she began spooning ground coffee into its tiny basket, she noticed something amiss. The entire heating element on the bottom of the unit had been removed, and the cord was missing as well. Smoke coming out of both ears, she picked up the phone, prepared to call home and confront The Beaver forthwith. Then, wearily shaking her head and trying to focus her caffeine-deprived eyes, she gave up and dialed room service instead.

"The percolator was beavered beyond repair..." she lamented, recalling the loss of the coffeemaker as though it were yesterday. Staring dreamily off into space, she went on. "You have no idea how embarrassing it was the time we had friends over to watch **Bonanza** on the new color TV we'd just bought the day before. Harold went to turn it on, and the picture tube was missing. We were nearly laughed out of the neighborhood."

Over the years, I had heard many stories about things The Beaver "appropriated," like the picture tube, the radios, vacuum cleaner motors, etc. But curiously, my in-laws didn't seem to know or care what had happened to their stolen property, and worse, acted as though they enjoyed relating The Beaver's youthful crimes. Things changed, however, when The Beav turned 16 and got his first jalopy, and parts started disappearing from their personal vehicles. At first it wasn't anything serious - a spark plug or two, a radio here and there. But when the oil pump went missing from his dad's Pontiac Grand Prix, the shit hit the fan, and The Beaver was rounded up and taken into custody.

"What do you know about this?" my father-in-law asked unsmilingly, positioning a desk lamp close to The Beaver's face."

"Golly gee whiz," The Beav said, his eyes wide with apprehension. Trying to conceal his grease-caked fingernails from his father's angry gaze, he mumbled. "I'm not sure what this is all about, Dad."

My father-in-law erupted. "You damn well ***do*** know what I'm talking about! You were out there in the garage all day yesterday with the doors locked. The Grand Prix was running fine yesterday morning, today it isn't. The oil pump's missing. Your clunker wasn't running yesterday. Today it is. There's oil spilled all over your parking spot in the driveway and oily footprints in your room. And look at your greasy fingernails!"

Evidence was rapidly mounting against The Beav, when my mother-in-law interrupted the interrogation. "Now, Harold," she scolded, "Stop badgering The Beaver. Why, Eddie Haskell was hanging out with Wally yesterday, and I saw Eddie go onto the garage. You know, as well-mannered as that young man is, I've never entirely trusted him. The Beaver's obviously protecting somebody," she said, comforting The Beav with a benevolent smile and a pat on the head.

"Gee golly whiz, Dad," The Beaver added, "M..m..mom's right. You ***are*** being kind of ***paranoid*** about this oil pump thing."

At that moment my father-in-law realized that all the evidence that pointed so clearly to The Beaver's guilt was worthless, and that he'd already lost the case. Reaching for the phonebook to find the number of the Pontiac dealership, he looked at The Beaver and shrugged. "Screw it," he said resignedly.

"Language!" my mother-in-law admonished him. "The Beaver has enough on his mind without having to listen to that kind of talk."

I am easily amused, I admit it. And I am particularly susceptible to vulgar noises, such as nose-blowing, loud belches, and the sound a fart makes when it slowly escapes the confines of a vinyl chair seat. This isn't something I'm necessarily proud of, but it is a trait I inherited from a long line of humorous folk who laugh at anything they find even moderately funny, and continue to do so until they piss (and sometimes even shit) themselves.

Since I started writing **Trailer Dogs**, I've probably soiled myself 20 or 30 times, reminiscing about the spine-tingling honks of noses, the haunting rumble of a belch, or the kazoo-like sound of flatulence at the dinner table. Ok… to be perfectly transparent, thinking about the nasty stuff other people do causes my bladder to divest itself of contents.

If provoked to hysterics by something that *really* amuses me, I may also fall to the floor and convulse and flop about the room until I land on a patch of carpet, limp, with tears streaming down my face and squelchy underwear. In anticipation of such events, I keep a spray bottle of Resolve Pet Stain Remover on hand at all times. It's not as simple when we're at a movie theater, visiting friends, or, attending the annual RV & Boat Show. I also make it a habit to carry several fresh pairs of underwear and a box of gallon-size Ziploc bags when we go anywhere that I might encounter something that strikes me funny.

It's a family curse. My older sister suffers the most from it. For certain reasons (one of her sons is a lawyer), I won't use her real name. But since she's 22 years older than me and has one foot in the grave, I think it's ok to refer to her by her family nickname, which is "Beanie."

Beanie is an extrovert and always has been. As the oldest of my siblings, she naturally puts herself in charge of everybody and everything, even though she barely tops 5'1, and, to put it as charitably as I am able, is shaped like one of those round-bottomed clown toys a baby can push, but never knock over. In her youth, Beanie was a stunner and had many suitors. That was before she got old, and her monstrous boobs fell to the floor and turned her into the above-mentioned clown toy.

Beanie is a talented, prize-winning artist. Her still life watercolors have taken first place at many art fairs and co-op gallery openings. She's very intelligent, and of all my siblings, she's the one I least like to play Scrabble with, and the ***only*** one I'm afraid to insult to her face. Beanie has another talent none of the rest of us were blessed with – that is, she can fart at will. Not only can Beanie work up a monster fart at a moment's notice, but like a veteran ventriloquist, she can make it seem to have come from twenty feet away.

I don't know how she does it. It's a gift from God. I've seen a group of party goers sniffing the air and glaring balefully at a beauty queen who minutes before had been the center of their attention, when a long, drawn-out fart seemed to wind its down from the skirt of her evening gown, and was now threatening to clear the room.

Beanie was so practiced and so competent at working her fart magic, that the beauty queen became red-faced, and apologized profusely for passing wind in mixed company. On the other side of the room, had anyone bothered to look, Beanie, the picture of innocence, would be inconspicuously fanning her backside and smiling broadly.

But getting back to the subject of terrible manners that provoke laughter, Beanie, like myself, is a victim of the family curse. When she hears a fart or belch, or particularly loud nose-blowing, she will often fall down in a fit of hysterics that result in the aforementioned pissing and/or shitting of herself. But the curse is a blade that can cut two ways, as Beanie found out early one morning about ten years back. The story is legend in our clan.

Beanie and her son, Jeffry, were on a road trip of sorts. Jeffry is a lawyer, and his court appearances often take him to the state capitol. Beanie likes to travel with Jeffry on those occasions, mainly because he pays for all her meals, entertainment, and puts her up at a nice hotel if they have to stay overnight.

Most of all, Beanie likes to go to court with Jeffry to see her boy, who she sometimes refers to as "little Jesus," get the best of other lawyers as he passionately defends drunks, petty thieves and deadbeat dads. Even though he's painfully thin and near-Albino pale, in Beanie's eyes, Jeffry's like the matchless hulking Raymond Burr as Perry Mason, astounding jurors and TV audiences alike with his brilliant legal mind.

Having left before dawn, mother and son were barreling down the interstate in Jeffrey's new Beamer. A fastidious young man, Jeffrey kept the leather interior of the car spotless. A full roll of paper towels was tucked behind the passenger's seat for emergency clean ups, and a dispenser of hand sanitizer was nearby in a compartment of the console. Beanie was slurping the last of the cola from her Big Gulp cup, and the Beamer's marvelous sound system was playing one of Jeffrey's favorite operas, when the fart materialized. Matching the soprano's crescendo in both pitch and volume, it filled the interior of the car with sounds not unlike the brass section's warm ups before a concert at Geffen Hall.

"God Almighty, Mother," Jeffry screamed, trying desperately to regain control of the Beamer's trajectory in time to avoid hitting the south-bound guardrail. "You'll kill us both!" Beanie, already experiencing laugh spasms and foaming slightly at the corners of her mouth, could not form the proper words to convey an apology. "Blehuh bhahahah" was all she managed to get out before the damn burst and she pissed all over the leather seat of Jeffry's new car.

Swerving off the freeway into a rest area, Jeffry roared to a stop in the parking lot, not too far from the bathrooms. The rest area was deserted, and the street lights were still on. "Get out" Jeffry commanded from between clenched teeth. Beanie got out of the car and headed toward the women's room, tossing the empty Big Gulp into a barrel beside a waist-high fence.

Inside, the rest room was empty, so she removed her pull-on slacks and rinsed the seat in one of the sinks. Then she slipped out of her sodden panties and put them in another sink, filling it with warm water and soap from the dispenser. Using a fist full of paper towels, she cleaned herself up as best she could. She put the slacks, still damp in the seat, back on, and stood in front of the hand dryer on tiptoes. While the slacks were drying, Beanie finished rinsing her panties and wrung them out.

Outside, Beanie hurried over to the Beamer where Jeffry was waiting impatiently, still mad as a hornet and worried that he was going to be late for court. He'd used up the roll of paper towels and hand sanitizer cleaning the passenger seat, and he was in no mood for civility. When Beanie approached the car, damp underwear in hand, he pressed the door lock and rolled the window down slightly. "No way you're bringing those disgusting things in here, Mother. Don't even think about it."

Beanie shrugged. The panties had been expensive as panties go, and she didn't really want to toss them in the trash barrel. But it appeared Jeffry was giving her no choice in the matter. Thinking that a homeless woman or perhaps an indiscreet, pantyless traveler might be able to use them, Beanie draped the freshly washed undies over the top of the split rail fence, where they hung in the morning air like a queen-size pillowcase on a clothesline.

Minutes later, as the Beamer raced down the freeway, Beanie began to fret over her lost panties. She'd paid good money for them, and they were her favorite, best-fitting pair. She didn't want to be responsible for Jeffry being late to court, but on the other hand, he ***had*** been uncharacteristically harsh with her back there at the rest stop. A sympathetic judge might even construe Jeffry's behavior as elder abuse.

After listening for almost 15 miles to his mother bemoaning her abandoned drawers, Jeffry turned the car around at the next exit and sped back to the rest stop full tilt boogie. The sun was up now, and groups of travelers had gathered, waiting to use the rest rooms, stretching their legs, and drinking coffee from lidded cups.

Screeching to a halt behind a van parked in front of the entrance, Jeffry kept the car running while Beanie hopped out. The panties were where she'd left them, fluttering slightly in the cool morning breeze.

Twenty pairs of eyes watched in disbelief as a petite, plump woman, with a dark wet stain in the seat of her slacks, jogged past them and plucked the giant drawers from the fence. Head held high, she jogged back to the waiting BMW. The last they saw of her, Beanie was waving the panties out an open window as the Beamer sped away.

"Did you see the way those people were staring at us, Mother?" Jeffry asked, glad to be back on the freeway once more. "I don't think I've been more embarrassed in my entire life. Not even that time you peed on the floor at Grandpa's funeral." At the memory of all the nose-blowing during her father-in-law's funeral, Beanie put her hand over her mouth, clenched her damp ass cheeks together, and began to cackle. Jeffry knew it was just a matter of time before he'd have to find another rest stop.

I suppose you're wondering what this interlude about Beanie has to do with what I put up with out of my old man on a daily basis. I will attempt to enlighten you by describing several of his worst flaws. Out of a sense of altruism, I won't include any more of his pathetic attempts on my life, and how he denies they even occurred by accusing me of being paranoid, which, as I've said before, makes him a big fucking liar in addition to everything else.

BIGGEST SLOB I'VE EVER KNOWN

Remember the old TV series **The Odd Couple,** with Tony Randall and Jack Klugman? I watched it every week for one reason alone: I had the hots for Randall's character, Felix Unger. Felix was everything a woman could want in a man.

Felix Unger was, to me anyway, deliciously handsome in a little-plastic-man-atop-the-wedding-cake-with-butter-frosting-on-his-feet sort of way. He was obsessively tidy, he was a gourmet cook, polite, perfectly groomed, respectful and sympathetic to women, and knowledgeable about art and literature. Hell, there was even a fifty-fifty chance he was gay, so he'd never disappoint a woman in the bedroom without makeup cuddling afterward. I was bewitched with longing for him.

Oscar Madison, on the other hand, was a train wreck. Jack Klugman, rest his soul, played Oscar, a cigar-smoking, sports-loving skirt chaser. Up until the day I saw my old man lick peanut butter off a knife and then toss the knife back in the silverware drawer, Oscar Madison was the biggest slob I'd ever known. Except for the cigar-smoking, sports-loving, and skirt chasing parts, my old man *is* Oscar Madison.

You will not meet anyone as disordered as my old man. He never closes a cabinet door or shuts a drawer, and when he rams into them 10 minutes later, he causes significant injury to either his head or his balls.

When this happens, as it does 2-3 times a day, he will rub the top of his head or clutch his groin and mutter "stupid fucking door/drawer" as though the jagged pain in his nutsack was caused by a lack of intelligence on the part of the inanimate object. Even then, he won't bother to shut the dim-witted offender, because, as he will surely tell you, "...I might have to get something out of there later on." He uses this same tactic on the even dumber refrigerator door, which he will leave hanging open until midnight, when he's ready to break out a six pack he's been chilling.

My old man's inability to aim his dick is the stuff legends are made of. He can't hit the center of a toilet bowl to save his goddamn life. You'd think an uncontrolled fire hose attached to the bladder of a bull moose got loose in our bathroom after he uses it.

This wasn't that much of a problem when we lived in a house that had more than one bathroom and we didn't have to share. Here in the trailer, it's a nightmare that never ends. I've begged him to sit down or at least clean up after himself, but he refuses. "It's not 'manly'," he tells me. Well, I got news for him. It's not "womanly" for me to use his green face towel to wipe piss off the walls and ceiling either.

Oh, and don't think I'm not sensing your negativity toward me, Dear Reader. Like I've said, I'm psycho, and I pick up on that kind of hostility.

Right now you're driving down the freeway in heavy traffic, texting snotty things about me with your bbf:

> Havu read abt her oman pizzen all ovr da broom
>
> Yah waz up wittat shit
>
> She da 1 bin pizzin on evrythg
>
> Yah her anner fubar sis lol
>
> Can we geddar mon back on buk

IYFD

Jus bak endd effn pikup truk bbl

Just so you know, Dear Reader, me and my so-called "Fucked Up Beyond All Repair" sister spend a lot of time CLEANING UP OUR OWN PISS. If you don't believe me, my old man will confirm it at the end of this chapter.* And also, why do you keep trying to pick fights with me? GAFL.

More evidence of my old man's sloppiness is on the bathroom mirror in the form of water spots, blobs of toothpaste, and on one occasion, a length of used dental floss that was dangling from the aforementioned blob of toothpaste. Don't ask me how the hell **that** happened. He thinks he's Michael Jordan when it comes to lobbing trash or garbage at the waste basket. Take my word on it. He's not Michael Jordan, unless maybe you're thinking about the Michael Jordan I went to grade school with, a kid so clumsy he chased after a baseball and fell into a goddamn dumpster.

ALL-TIME WORST DRESSER

This one probably should have been combined with Biggest Slob, but sometimes a writer gets confused about having to insert so many paragraphs in different places after she's had a box or two of wine. Listing all my old man's faults has to cover a lot of ground. I'm not sure what I meant by that last sentence, but like I said, box wine. Also, I'm kind of tired and wasted right now, so you'll just have to figure it out for yourself. I can't be held responsible for what you read here.

When my old man takes off his clothes, he doesn't hang them up so much as he wads them into big wrinkly, sweaty balls, and stuffs them in the back of the closet. Again, this wasn't as much of a problem when we lived in a house and each of us had our own closet. Sharing a closet with my old man in a trailer is like sharing a midden with a packrat. Unless I fumigate it several times a week and toss his wretched balls into the laundry basket, our closet smells like Shrek's armpits on a hot summer day.

FYI: *A packrat's midden, or nest, is composed of sticks, twigs, rotted plant materials, turds, and copious amounts of the packrat's own urine to hold the mess together.*

If I didn't keep track of and supervise our laundry, God knows what my old man would wear to work every day. It's bad enough as it is. He can have 5 clean dresss shirts and a new pair of slacks hanging in the closet, and he'll still fish around in the back until he snags an old tee with dried dog puke on the front, and a hole the size of Uranus on the back. He'll pair the foul tee with the same deep-cut cotton breeches he wore working the plow back yonder in the Oregon Territory, and he's all set to go.

Just last Saturday we were about to head out to the grocery when I noticed the shorts he was wearing (with black calf-length socks and sandals) had dried red paint on the ass, and what appeared to be the upper half of a frog's corpse stuck near the right side pocket. "Forget it. I'm not leaving here with you dressed like that," I told him.

"There's nothing wrong with what I have on," he glowered, screwing up his face like Trump does when he thinks somebody's about to step on his nuts. "These are my weekend play clothes."

"Yeah, you look like you've been playing with explosives in a swamp," I retorted, eyeing the ripped pocket on the polo shirt he'd selected to complete his ensemble. He always pulls that "play clothes" crap, like he has a whole other Arnold Palmer brand wardrobe he can yank from the closet when he's late for tee time at Pebble Beach. "Get in there and put on something decent, and this time don't get it out of the fucking rag bin."

He huffed back into the bedroom and rummaged around in the closet for a minute or two, then came back out. This time the shorts he had put on were so wrinkled they looked like a relief map of Afghanistan, and his tee shirt was so old, it had "Say Hello to Pan Am" printed on the chest. He'd exchanged the sandals for white sneakers, but kept the black socks. "I give up, wear what you want," I relented, "But don't expect to have lunch *inside* at Mickey Ds. We'll be using the drive-thru today."

A PIG HAS BETTER MANNERS

It's a terrible burden, having to write these disgusting things about a man I've been married to since before Yoko broke up the Beatles, but my readers demand the truth. My old man can't go 5 minutes without farting or belching or scratching something so far down in his crotch, his elbow gets caught in his waistband. I think the belching is maybe the worst of the lot.

When we were still living in our house, our closest neighbors were about a quarter mile away. One fine sunny morning I was at the kitchen window, looking through binoculars at our neighbor, who was up on his roof, shirtless, and making repairs. As he crossed back and forth along the roof's peak, I kept the binocs trained on his muscular form in case he fell and I had to run down there and perform CPR on him.

I had just finished adjusting the binocs' magnification, when my old man came into the room, scratching his beer belly and sniffing the air for any trace of Cinnabons. All at once he began a belch -perhaps the loudest in his long, sordid history of belching. I watched through the binoculars as our neighbor's head snapped around in the direction of our house. The roar of the belch had startled him even at that great distance. He fell on his ass and began a perilous slide toward the eaves.

"Where ya goin'?" my old man wanted to know as I shoved past him.

"Bathroom," I choked. "Gotta take a shower and change my pants."

I can't speak to her sister, Beanie's, behavior, but Ellen's telling the truth when she says she spends hours cleaning up her own pee. She did make one small error - maybe because she's slightly color blind: The green towel she's been using to clean around the toilet is her face towel. Mine's the blue one.

Joke's on you, pally boy. Just wait until everybody sees the wall-pissing picture of you in Trailer Dogs.

My Old Man

CHAPTER 11

THE FOURTH ESTATE, DOG STYLE

Trailer Dog Media

News spreads fast here at the Resort. Whether it's a recap of Gretchen and Lloyd's latest brawl, or a report on overnighters that were caught letting their dog swim in the pool, every long-term resident will have heard about it by the end of the day.

A lot of times it's like the kids' game "Telephone." The original report may start out as: "Two sheriff's deputies were seen patrolling the park last night." By the time the last person hears the story, it likely will have mutated into: "Two little green men in a UFO probed Gerald in his big dumb ass last night."

Lonnie May, of course, is the primary source of gossip and information for the park, and he covers every beat, from national politics and the local police blotter, to economics, climate science and medical breakthroughs. His storylines and reporting are heavily influenced by his dedication to conservative talk radio. With Daisy May at his side, he makes his rounds through the park like the Village Limbaugh.

"Now, take old Bernie Sanders…" he'll say to a rapt gathering of Trailer Dogs. "The guy's a straight up Commonest. I seen a pitcher of him eatin' Mex food with Castro. Obama was in there too. I *seen* it. Sanders don't believe in no God. He's a Muslin like Obama. Neither one of them guys believe in God and Jesus. That's why they made are kids stop prayin' in school."

After he's said his piece, Lonnie invariably pauses to assess audience reaction. "Did you *know* that?" he'll ask them. Heads will shake thoughtfully, pondering whether or not they had known it before Lonnie reported it.

Lonnie does not like to be confronted or contradicted with facts or other information. After downing a few beers, one of his buddies, Ernie, dared to challenge him: "Hey, Lon, I heard on the TV old Bernie Sanders is a Jew. He ain't no Muslin like Obama."

Lonnie fixed his pal with a dismissive smirk. "All them Muslins is from the Middle East, and that makes 'em Jews by birth. It's right there in your Bible, Ern, if your worthless old ass would read it."

Ern drained his beer and tossed the empty can in the vicinity of the garbage pail. It missed, and clanked against the side of our trailer. "Hell, I didn't *know* that," he admitted. "Old Bernie Sanders ain't even a American, but at least he ain't no *black* Jew Muslin like Obama!"

The "hoax" of Global Warming is another subject dear to Lonnie's heart. In January, he was harping about it to a few of his buddies, who'd stopped by to get drunk and transact whatever "business" Lonnie conducts with them during the week. I could hear his loud, gravelly voice through the thin walls of our trailer.

"Man, it was cold last night. Me and Daisy May 'bout froze our asses off, didn't we, Daisy May? Old Al Gore thought he could pull a fast one on us about them glacier's meltin' and drownin' everbody and it gettin' too hot. Them glaciers is actually getting' *bigger* all the time. I *seen it* on TV. That's what's causin' all them polar bears to die out. They can't get in the ocean to eat fish for all that froze ice. I seen a polar bear on TV and it was *layin' on the ice*, starved to death. Wolves were eatin' on it. Old Al Gore wants us to think them bears died of Global Warmin' so he can sell more of his damn solar panels."

Long pause. "Did you *know* that?"

Lonnie's soapbox opinions wouldn't be complete without a dimwitted jab at the gay and Lesbian communities.

"God done made men and women differnt so they could profligate. There ain't no such thing as two guys or two gals marryin' in the eyes of the Lord. They can't profligate. It's abdominal for a man to lay with another man. That's right there in your Bible."

A couple of Lonnie's long-term bachelor pals may look a mite uncomfortable, but no one in the audience owns a Bible, or would be willing to stop swilling free beer long enough to look up an exact citation. The asinine assertion goes unchallenged.

One afternoon, Lonnie, agitated and minus Daisy May, banged on our door. "I just come over to give you a heads up," he said a little breathlessly. "In about two weeks the whole damn country's gonna have a economic collapse. Did you *know* that?"

I confessed that I did not. "Yep, the whole damn thing. The goverment's out of money and ain't gonna print no more. There won't be no food in the stores and no banks. We're gonna have another grave depression. The stock market's gonna collapse and we're all gonna lose money on it."

I was a little skeptical. "You have money in the stock market?"

"Aw, hell no! I don't got no money nowhere, not after today" he grunted, "I went out and bought Daisy May 40 pounds of food and filled up the truck. We're all set. And you better be doin' the same. Get a bunch of food laid in for yer dogs. I don't like to say this, but when things get real bad, I ain't gonna be able to share any of Daisy May's food with nobody, no matter what."

"How long is this crisis supposed to last, Lonnie?"

"Maybe months, maybe years," he said, rubbing the back of his grimy neck. "It's Obama's deal. We'll be ok here at the park 'cause we have a lot of ex-military and the like with weapons, and the dogs'll warn us when strangers come around. They's wild turkeys and rabbits in them hills, so we're gonna organize huntin' parties."

"Gerald might be the one to put in charge of that," I suggested, "I heard he's a pretty good hunter."

Lonnie became visibly irritated. "Old Gerald don't know squat about shit," he said hotly. "He ain't fit to run nothin' except for his big mouth. And he ain't no hunter neither. He bought most of them antlers off some other guy. Did you **know** that?" Completely forgetting about the imminent collapse of the national economy, Lonnie continued to rant about Gerald.

"That son of bitch hollered at Daisy May for gettin' in his goddamn horn pile. We went by there one time and he had all that shit layin' around, and Daisy May went up and helped herself to a horn. She had that big old horn in her mouth and was walkin' around proud-like, and Gerald come runnin' out screamin' like a banshee and chasin' after her like she done stole his pickup. He wouldn't have pulled that shit on my old Rambo, I'll tell you that right now. Old Rambo woulda tore his ass off and had it for supper."

"Who's Rambo?" I asked, glad that the state of the US economy was momentarily off the agenda, and I was about to hear what was perhaps a human interest story.

Lonnie drew a deep breath. "Back when I was still workin' and livin' in a reglar house - way before Daisy May - I had me a heeler named Rambo. Old Rambo, he was a bad-ass alright." Lonnie chuckled at the memory.

"That fuckin' dog could jump over fences 10 feet high, and tunnel like you wouldn't believe. I couldn't keep a leash on him. He wouldn't go for that leash, no way. I got in trouble with the law a couple times over him gettin' in people's yards and maulin' and attackin' them and their kids and pets, but nothin' ever come of it."

"What happened to old Rambo?" I asked, sensing there was more to the sad tale.

Lonnie wrinkled his brow and became pensive. "I never was for sure, but I got home from work one day and found him layin' out in the back yard with a bullet in his brain. Saddest day of my life. It about killed me, losing that dog. There's a lot of crazy asses and dog haters in this world." *And a lot of them want to punch us in our throats, I thought to myself.*

As you may already have surmised, Dear Reader, the US economy never totally collapsed as Lonnie predicted, but some damn heavy chunks of it fell on us and sent us reeling. Trailer Dogs, being more or less used to a daily battering from economic shit storms, limped along and somehow got by.

Having spent all his money on supplies for a disaster that never fully materialized, Lonnie asked to borrow 100 bucks to tide him over. I gave him $50, not because I felt sorry for him, but because I figured he'd just show up every day asking to "borrow" lunchmeat and dog food for him and Daisy May.

This all happened about the same time Gerald bought a lottery scratch ticket and won $500,000. The whole Resort was abuzz with the great news, except for Lonnie. He was so uncharacteristically tight-lipped about it, you'd have thought he was Trump at an IRS audit.

Most everybody in the park figured Gerald would use the windfall to buy a little house of his own, somewhere near his mother. That speculation died when a boom truck pulled up in front of his junky old trailer, and four steel beams were planted at each corner. Not long after that, workmen came and attached large sheets of canvas to the roof of the structure. The two long sides of the trailer were outfitted with sunshades that could be raised or lowered, and the ends of the giant "rigport" were left open so the trailer could be moved out, if desired. The pile of antlers and horns remained undisturbed by the installation work.

Other improvements to Gerald's site soon followed. The crooked wooden steps were removed, and a small deck with a ramp, obviously to facilitate Lulu's path to the ground, stood in their place. A brand new deluxe gas barbeque replaced the two greasy ones, and the mismatched fence, still half finished, was dismantled and hauled away. Stacks of new fence sections were delivered from Lowes, and were awaiting Gerald's attention. His old Ford pickup was still parked next to the trailer, and was sporting a new set of tires.

As I walked the boys past Gerald's place one morning, Lulu was at the window looking as adorable as ever. Gerald's site, however, looked pretty much the same as it had before. Unfinished projects had been relocated to the new deck, and most of the crap he'd had scattered around was still there. Somebody said he'd used most of his lottery winnings to put his mother in a fancy assisted-living complex, but I didn't believe that for a second. It seemed more likely that Gerald would use the money to set up a trust fund for Lulu. She is, after all, his only child.

CHAPTER 12

THE BIG STINK

Once he saw that Gerald wasn't going to use his lottery winnings to buy the Resort from its current owners and throw him and Daisy May out on their asses, Lonnie regained his chatty cynicism and resumed his doomsday outlook about the economy, gay marriage, immigration, climate change, and Mexicans (plotting to take good jobs away from him that he wasn't qualified for in the first place). He knew I went past Gerald's every morning, and he was always fishing for information about what his nemesis was up to.

"Gerald's building a shed over there," I told him one afternoon, as Daisy May sniffed around our site, looking for a convenient place to take a dump. She circled about a dozen times before situating herself over the chosen target.

Lonnie snorted. "That shit fer brains don't know one end of a hammer from the other," he said, reaching for the bill of his baseball cap with the remaining thumb and two fingers on his left hand.

"Gerald's hiring it done," I informed him. "There were some carpenters over there this morning, and they were about to finish it up. Looks pretty solid." I couldn't resist. "Did you *know* that?"

Maybe because he hadn't known about Gerald's new shed and was embarrassed at my having scooped him on the story, a few weeks later Lonnie couldn't wait to report some upsetting news he'd learned through the park grapevine.

"Did you hear about Gretchen and the big stink over by dumbass Gerald's?"

I admitted I was in the dark. "Was somebody late paying their rent?" *I knew Gretchen turned into Dragon Lady if anyone's rent was a couple days overdue.*

"Naw, nothin' like that," Lonnie said, impatiently waving off my guess. "This deal was with the old guy that moved in the spot where that lady in the Winnebago used to be. You know, the gal Gretchen kicked out for havin' three cats? Over there by Gerald." *Ah...so it was the cat lady's replacement who caused a ruckus with Gretchen. Always interested in karmic payback, I bade Lonnie continue.*

"It all started when the old guy calls Gretchen and tells her the sewer connection on his fiver is bad and leakin' or some shit. He has to leave messages 'cause Gretchen never answers the fuckin' phone, and anyhow, she never calls him back. Finally, he goes on down to the office and tells Gretchen she better do somethin' about it quick, 'cause it's stinkin' up the whole block. She tells him Lloyd'll come over and have a look, like that would help, since fuckin' Lloyd don't know his ass from a hole in the head. Anyhow, old Lloyd never goes over, and everbody is complainin' more and more about the smell, asshat Gerald included."

This part of Lonnie's story rang an unpleasant bell. I'd noticed a nauseating odor wafting around Gerald's neighborhood when I walked the boys, but had attributed it to the Canadians' dumpster. Now that I thought about it, the corn holing season was over, and all the Canadians had come and gone.

"So old Lloyd never goes over, and a week goes by, and Gerald tells Gretchen he's callin' the county health department if she don't take care of it 'cause the stench is even puttin' Lulu off her chow. Gretchen gets on the warpath and hustles on over to the guy's trailer, but he ain't around, and the smell is so bad she can't hardly stand it. She bangs on the door and then opens it 'cause the dumbass guy left it unlocked. She goes in there, and the stink nearly makes her pass out.

She goes on into the bedroom, and there the old guy is, laid out on the bed, dead as shit, flies buzzin' all over him. Gretchen turns around to run out of there and falls down the step and breaks her fuckin' ankle! hahahaha, hoohoohoo! I wisht I coulda been there to see the look on her face when she seen that dead guy hahahaha.. and then she falls on her ass and breaks her leg because of the stink…hahahaha!" Lonnie was laughing so hard, he couldn't breathe. "Oh Lord, talk about your eye for eye and tooth for tooth, hahahaha!"

Even though it involved Gretchen getting some well-deserved comeuppance and even though I'm notorious for laughing at just about anything that doesn't involve kids or animals getting hurt, I was having trouble finding humor in the death of an old man who'd spent his last few days in the back of a hot trailer, tormented by a stinking sewer connection.

"You know, Lonnie," I ventured, "That poor old man deserved better than to die alone in his trailer like that. It could happen to any of us." *I thought, but did not say, that it could especially happen to somebody like Lonnie, who didn't have any family or real friends looking out for him.* "Maybe the whole thing isn't all that funny."

Lonnie became contemplative for a few moments before he spoke again.

"I wasn't makin' fun of the old dead guy," he said, "I didn't know the man. But it was about time Gerald got his just deserves for puttin' that big fancy roof over his fiver and actin' like he can boss everbody around since he won all that money. Anyhow, there's no call for you to go judgin' me and shit. ***Judge not, less ye'll be judged.*** That's right there in your Bible." With no Bible at hand, and no desire to parse what he'd just said, I had to let Lonnie's admonishment go unchallenged.

Without Canadian Ian to make his dutiful wife help her, and her ankle in a cast, Gretchen had serious problems with performing her Resort management duties, particularly keeping track of which residents were breaking the rules and which ones she could bully into ratting out the offenders. It was summer, and Lloyd Bird had his hands full supervising the pool area, so he was of even less use than usual, which is to say he was well into minus territory as far as being of any use whatsoever.

On the way to the laundry room one morning, I was shocked to see Lonnie vacuuming the carpet in the clubhouse, and on my way out I ran into him again, this time mopping the hallway by the bathrooms. "What's up, Lonnie?" I asked, "Gretchen paying you to help out while her ankle heals?" His face reddened.

"Naw, she ain't payin' me nothin'. I just offered to help out around here a little." This sudden act of kindness didn't sound a thing like the Lonnie I knew and didn't like. Something was rotten in the state of Denmark, and I was going to find out what it was. "Well, you ought to be getting paid **something** for your work, Lonnie. Otherwise people might think you're a Commonist."

Lonnie screwed up his face and snorted. "You know the trailer that old guy died in? Well, none of his kin want it, what with him stinkin' it up like he done. It's a purty nice rig - bigger and newer than my fiver. Gretchen said if I did some chores until her ankle gets better, she might think about lettin' me swap it for my fiver."

"My God, Lonnie, what about the smell in that disgusting thing?"

Lonnie looked a little miffed. "Hey - -my fiver don't smell that bad no more," he said, a touch of resentment in his voice.

"Noooo, not **your** fiver. I mean the trailer that man died in – how could anybody live in it?"

"Oh yeah,-**that** fiver," Lonnie said, his face brightening. "See, that's the deal. I'm fixin' to clean it and fumigrade it so it's fit for human consumption. Then Gretchen might let me swap it, and she'll rent my fiver out to overnighters."

God help me, I could actually see the logic in this idea. Gretchen was going to have a hell of a time renting out the dead man's trailer, what with all the gossip that would be circulating about it for years to come. And ironically, Lonnie's broken down old 5th wheel wasn't in any worse shape than some of the other rentals at the Resort.

The more I thought about it, the more I warmed to the idea. The best thing about it was that Lonnie would be moving to another part of the Resort, and we could stay put at our current site. But wait! There might be a fly in the appointment as Lonnie would say. If the swap went through, he'd be living a couple sites down from his sworn enemy, Gerald. How was that going to work?

"What about Gerald being your neighbor?" I asked, barely concealing my fear that this was going to be the deal breaker. "Don't you two hate each other?"

"Awww hell no," Lonnie drawled. "Gerald's ok. We had our differnces, but now we git along just fine."

"I'm glad you patched things up with him," I said. "I hope the trailer swap works out. And I really mean that from the bottom of my heart," I told him. "Do to others like they do to you."

Over the next few weeks, Lonnie worked tirelessly at Deadman's Curb, as we'd all begun to call the site where the old fellow passed away. With steam cleaning equipment and a respirator rented by Gretchen, he went over the trailer inch by inch, until every trace of the morgue smell was gone. Then, wearing heavy gloves and a surgical mask, he tackled the sewer connection and repaired that. When Dr. May was finished with his treatments, Deadman's Curb was issued a clean bill of smell.

In the end, however, the swap never happened. Somebody offered Gretchen $10,000 for the dead man's trailer, and she snatched it up faster than a congressman accepts a bribe from a lobbyist. Lonnie wasn't all that unhappy with the collapse of the deal. Gretchen paid him $1,000 for his work on the trailer, which he promptly spent on scratch tickets, hoping to successfully duplicate Gerald's lucky strike. I think he ended up with about $75 in profit, and bragging rights for having "conned" Gretchen out of a thousand bucks, which was no mean feat for a Trailer Dog.

You may not think buying scratch tickets was the smart thing for Lonnie to do with his hard-earned cash, but as a wise guy once said: ***Judge not, less ye'll be judged.*** That's right there in your Bible.

EPILOG

Gretchen & Lloyd Bird

Gretchen's ankle finally healed. During her recovery, she slept on a sofa bed in the Resort's office so she wouldn't have to navigate the steps inside and outside the Birds' 5th wheel trailer. The arrangement apparently had the blessing of the Resort's absent owners, who live in another state, and who are content to leave the entire operation of the park in Gretchen's fists.

The office is equipped with a small kitchen and a half bath, and is a part of the Clubhouse, with its fireplace, billiards table, laundry facilities and showers. The one thing Gretchen's office lacks is Lloyd Bird, who avoids his wife at all costs, lest she find some task for him that will interrupt his liesure."

Gretchen liked the interim accommodations so much that she seems to have made them permanent. Rumor has it that she and the Bird's dog, Charles, are living in the office together, and Lloyd stays in their 5th wheel, cooking his own meals and probably looking at porn on the internet when he's not prowling around the pool. The only confirming evidence I have as to the validity of the rumor is the notable absence of the sign that formerly hung on the door to Gretchen's office:

NO SMOKING

&

ABSOLUTELY NO PETS ALLOWED

Ian Reeve & Mrs. Reeve (The Canadians)

Ian won't be coming back to the park this winter. I learned this in a roundabout way when we walked by the corn hole court one morning, and two husky-looking guys were dismantling it. When I took our rent check to the office, I asked Gretchen about it. She was seated in a high-back executive's chair, and Charles was beside her, occupying a chair of his own. Something about the pair reminded me of Dr. Evil and Mr. Bigglesworth.

"I decided it was time to get rid of that piece of shit corn hole court," Gretchen said decisively. "Nobody but the Canadian guys used it, and they're not even here most of the year. I'm thinking of putting in something everybody could use and enjoy. Maybe a shuffleboard court."

"Ian's going to be pretty disappointed," I observed. "Do Canadians play shuffleboard?"

"Who gives a shit what Ian plays?" Gretchen snapped. "Besides, he isn't coming back this year, praise God. Janet divorced him, and she got their motor home in the settlement."

This news came as a shock. For some time I'd suspected Gretchen and Ian were hooking up. He seemed to be in her office *a lot*. And he was always sending his wife (Janet?) over to help Gretchen out or to bring her food. Gretchen now seemed pretty hostile toward him. Could it have something to do with his fixation on the sport of corn holing?

I hustled on down to Virginia Lopps' to share the news. "I was gob smacked," I told her over a tall glass of Long Island Iced Tea. "I thought for sure Gretchen and Ian were doing the deed - the way he hung around the office so much and sucked up to her all the time while his poor dumb wife did all the shit work."

"Oh, boy, you sure got your signals mixed on that one, girl!" Virginia roared. "Ian wasn't shacking up with Gretchen, it was the other way around. Ian's wife, Janet, was the one shacking up with Gretchen!" I almost swallowed an ice cube. "What the fuuu…?" I choked. "You *cannot* be serious."

"Serious as a turd on the end of your fork," Virginia said, pouring more tea into my glass. "Gretchen put Ian in charge of the office every time she took a notion to "visit" Janet - and her and Janet got together in Gretchen's office every time Ian sent Janet over to clean something or do a favor for Gretchen. Those two old gals was thick as thieves. Everybody knew about it, honey."

"Lloyd?"

"Well sure…Lloyd don't give a shit as long as he can hang out around the pool gapin' at teenie boppers."

"And Ian knew?"

"I guess Ian didn't catch on until one night he finished up his corn holin' early, and walked in on Gretchen and Janet lovin' it up in the middle of his bed."

"How did you find out about all this, Virginia?" I asked, my head spinning from the revelation and her lethal tea.

"Oh, I got my sources," she said mysteriously. "Gretchen ain't the only one with spies in this goddamn place. And by the way, it wasn't Janet that filed for divorce on Ian, it was Ian who filed. He got their big house in Ontario, and she got the motor home. She may be comin' back here for keeps this year."

Unless we can get that damn wall built on the Canadian border, I thought.

"Resort Management"

Lonnie & Daisy May

Not a single thing has changed with Lonnie and Daisy May, not even Lonnie's filthy stinking clothes. In fact, the Mays are probably the most doting pair in the whole Resort, not counting Gerald and Lulu, of course. Lonnie still doesn't keep Daisy May on a leash, nor does he clean up after her, in complete disregard of Gretchen's rules. Nobody's turned him in yet, and it wouldn't do any good anyway, because since she's been living at the office with Charles, Gretchen not only ignores phone messages, she keeps the door locked during business hours.

Phyllis & Bill Crane

The Cranes are home in Montana now, after visiting their son in Chicago. While they were there, their son talked Phyllis into buying a smart phone. Then he made the huge mistake of teaching his tech-illiterate mom how to send a text message. I've had 11 from her in the last two days. Here is one of the *less* wordy ones:

hello there we are back in montana enjoying the summer weather everything is in bloom and it hasn't rained much so i am able to work in my garden whenever i want bill is helping me with the vegetables and he is working to fix the timers for the sprinklers and wishes your husband was here to help with it because of the good job your husband did on our wiring at the resort speaking of which bill wonders if your husband would go down and take a look and make sure our sprinklers are coming on at the right time and if not would he repair them and send us the bill or call somebody to repair them and pay for it and send us the bill i hope you and your dogs are having a nice summer and it is not too hot if it is hot and our sprinklers aren't working could you water our vines the hose is back in the secret garden and the water is turned on so be sure to turn it off after you water the plants thank you so much we cant wait to see you in november love phyllis and bill ps could you text me some pictures of my vines so i can make sure everything is ok thank you so much love phyllis and bill pss bill says hi love phyllis and bill text me back and i will answer you right away if im not driving love phyllis

Gerald & Lulu Karn

Even though his lottery win made him a one-percenter by Trailer Dog standards, Gerald kept his old rig with its new rigport. He finally got the storage shed assembled, but it must be empty, because his site looks more cluttered and worse than ever.

The horns and antlers are still lying around haphazardly, and it appears Gerald has a new hobby, turning them into table lamps. Several of the lamps are half-finished, and are lined up on his new deck with lopsided shades attached. They look dangerous, as if one might be impaled when reaching for the switch in the middle of the night. The paint cans and the lidless bins, overflowing with God-knows-what, are still there, and he never did finish that fence.

Remarkably, Gerald has turned out to be the Warren Buffet of the Resort's Trailer Dogs. Unbeknownst to everyone (except maybe Virginia Lopp) Gerald was the one who bought the dead guy's trailer from Gretchen for 10K. He then sold his mother's house for $300,000, which he banked. He moved the little old lady into the trailer on Deadman's Curb, two sites down from his own residence, and bought her an electronic keyboard.

Every Tuesday when her Bible study group meets, hymns radiate from within. Sometimes Lulu's happy face can be seen looking out the window at Grandma's trailer. The little Bichon is still horribly overweight from all the treats, and she's also still on my "Dogs I'd like to Kidnap" list. ***Forgive me, Lord, but when it comes to Bee-john Freezays, I just can't help myself.***

Marv & Patty Greer

No one has heard from the Greers, but their 5th wheel trailer is still parked in the site behind ours, its tires protected from the sun's harmful rays with white canvas covers. Patty and Marv will probably be back here come October, providing Patty isn't already in prison for disfiguring Marv with her teeth.

The Lopp Girls

The Lopps are doing great. Claudia is redecorating her park model with Native American style furnishings, and she recently completed an overhaul of her site's landscaping. She had a gorgeous new deck and steps built, and to the amazement of everyone, Gerald did the carpentry work. This might explain why his own landscaping projects have suffered. Bits and pieces of lumber left over from Claudia's deck are in little piles around his site. Just the other day I saw Lulu carrying a chunk of wood in her mouth as she waddled toward her Grandma's.

Laurette Lopp has acquired more gee gaws for her site, including a 6-foot high metal cactus, which she draped creatively with multi colored Christmas lights, and then ringed with plastic gnomes at the base. Laurette cut open the bottoms of the gnomes and put lights inside them. The display is semi horrific in the daylight, and fully horrific at night, when the lights come on and give the gnomes' misshapen faces a sinister, evil glow. Virginia's biding her time, just waiting for Gretchen to say one word about it.

Virginia Lopp still sits on her porch every day, drinking whiskey and keeping an eye on the comings and goings in Trailer Dog World. If it isn't too warm out, she has Princess, her cat, sitting on her lap. I have decided that Princess is Queen of the Trailer Cats. Since there aren't any other cats living in the Resort at this time, I guess she's actually Queen of the Trailer Dogs as well.

Cripple Jon

Cripple Jon and Maria are no longer an item. According to Lonnie, the breakup was because Maria is looking for somebody to marry who's a lot richer and handsomer than Cripple Jon.

Jon is back to rolling around the Resort spouting off about "beanerth" and "wetbackth," which may help explain why he bungled a job interview for a desk job at local tire distributor owned by third generation Mexican-Americans.

When we went to the local Credit Union last week, we were directed to the office of the Manager of New Accounts. When the Manager came in, we were bowled over. It was Maria. She immediately recognized us from the Resort, and told us that her father lives in the trailer park across the highway, with her invalid mother and their Australian heeler. Maria goes there often to clean their trailer and help care for her mother.

Before her job at the credit union started absorbing so much of her time, Maria was a volunteer at Meals on Wheels. That's how she met Cripple Jon – delivering his hot meals and helping him with various household chores. She met Lonnie when her dad bought some of Lonnie's tools at a swap meet, and Maria brought over her mom's homemade tamales for her Dad's lunch. He shared them with Lonnie, and Lonnie liked them so much, Maria's mother had Maria take a half-dozen to him at his trailer.

Maria said that she feels very badly for Lonnie and for Cripple Jon because of their unfortunate circumstances, but that her job and family occupy most of her time these days. She's happily married to a paramedic, and they're raising three children. And by her own admission, Maria makes really lousy tamales.

Me and My Old Man

 Five years ago if you'd told me I'd be living full time in a travel trailer in an RV park with two dogs, a husband who's been trying to kill me for decades, and neighbors, most of whom think America's Gross National Product is Brussels sprouts, I would have called you nuckin' futz. (As I've said, I wasn't as overtly profane as I am today.) I would have pointed out that our small business was growing steadily, we lived modestly, worked hard as we always had, and we still had sweat equity in our home despite the housing market crash.

 Five years ago we were confident that somehow, by some miraculous act of conscience, our government would find a way to rescue the American middle class from the edge of the abyss that the government itself had created through unnecessary wars, tax breaks for the super-rich, and an unregulated Wall Street so out of control, it awarded millions in bonuses to the very people who'd masterminded the excavation of the abyss.

 Five years ago we didn't realize that we were part of the middle class that had already toppled over the edge of the chasm, and that we, along with millions of other Americans, were dangling by one hand from a limb that was already broken.

 Five years ago we couldn't imagine that the U.S. Government would shut itself down, that orders for our products would be cancelled, and that we'd lose our business, our life savings, and most of the equity in our house. If we had foreseen it, we might not have been so naive as to keep trying to hold onto that broken limb.

Five years ago we didn't realize that the "abyss" wasn't really an "abyss" at all. It was just a new reality for middle class Americans like us, a challenge we could accept or simply ignore, in which case we might just as well sit down and wait to die. It took us a while, but in the end, as disappointed and disillusioned as we felt, we chose not to give up on ourselves.

If we are nothing else, Trailer Dogs, regardless of our race, gender, IQ, sexual orientation, or country of origin, are **survivors**. We've helped to shape America from the ground up. We've traveled dangerous paths across oceans and hostile territories, and have suffered countless deprivations and injustices. We've faced one obstacle after another, not always pulling in the same direction at the same time, but with the same goal of making a better life for our families, and for generations of Americans yet to come.

So, here we are, me and my old man, almost three years after we let go of the broken limb and fell head-first into Trailer Dog World. Gone are the trappings of suburbia, the things we'd been absolutely certain we couldn't get along without, and the hell we'd been putting ourselves through trying to live the non-existent "American Dream." We now live in a real neighborhood, made up of interesting, unconventional characters - some of them even loonier than we are. The playing field, though it may be mined with Daisy May's poop from time to time, is a lot more level.

We have each other and we have our boys. Believe it or not, we're not only happy, we feel better and more optimistic about the future than we have in our entire lives. A trailer park is a great place to raise dog kids without worrying about getting punched in the throat for the privilege. And speaking of getting punched in the throat for treating dogs like people, it's a risk I'm more than willing to take. I love our Trailer Dog boys with all my heart and all my soul. And I love my old man just as much.

Ben & Sully

A MESSAGE FROM THE AUTHOR

When I decided to write *Trailer Dogs*, it was more as a cathartic exercise than anything else. We'd suffered some devastating blows, and I was a cauldron of raw nerves and bitterness, with a dash of Irish fatalism thrown in.

As I pondered exactly what was on my mind and what I wanted to say in the book about our offbeat new life in a trailer park, I started to worry about what readers – if there were any – might think of me, and what kind of reception a book about coping with what I saw as personal failure, would receive.

I was afraid. I was afraid to share some of our ego-crushing experiences and missteps with strangers, even when cast in a humorous light. More than that, I was afraid that few would understand the book, or worse, would misinterpret what I had written.

Then one day I asked myself: *What would Cheekly, the bravest rescue Chihuahua who ever lived, have done?*

Hope you enjoyed *Trailer Dogs*, folks, and thanks for reading!

Ellen

PLEASE ADD YOUR REVIEW!

Now that you have completed *Trailer Dogs*, we hope you will leave a review so that other readers may benefit from your perspective. Authors like Ellen Garrison live and die by your reviews, after all!

To share your reading experience with the author of Trailer Dogs, please visit

https://www.amazon.com/dp/B01DKRPGBC

COMING IN MAY 2017

Revenge of the Trailer Dogs:
Life in America's New Middle Class
By Ellen Garrison

ADVANCE CRITICISMS

Her first book was terrible, and I hated this one even worse, which is why I didn't read either one of them. And by the way, why wasn't there anything about the Bowling Green Massacre in these books?   *Kellyanne Conway*

Somebody said she mocked me in her first book, but I'm pretty sure it wasn't me she was making fun of. I am a Brain Surgeon and I know many things about Egyptian storage containers.   *Ben Carson, Dr./Secretary/World Authority on Grain Storage/Author of Gifted Hams*

That gal ain't a African American is she? Seems like that gal might be a African American. Y'all call my office if urinall have any information on that gal.   *J. Sessions*

This woman very bad person. This woman say things in her book she will regret.   *V. Putin, President of the United States of Russia.*

Another book about things and chumps I have zero interest in, especially now that the election's over.   *DJT, Co-Prez of the United States of Russia*

Man, I wish I'd had the balls to say some of the stuff in both of those books.   *Little Marco Rubio*

Man, I wish I'd had the credibility to say some of the stuff in both of those books.   *JEB!*

Ditto on both counts.   *Lyin' Ted Cruz*

I *had* the balls to say some of the stuff in both of those books, and all it got me was a crappy lunch with the asshole.   *Mitt*

http://www.trailerdogs.net

Made in the USA
Monee, IL
14 July 2021